TERRORISM EXPLAINED

The facts about terrorism and terrorist groups

Clive Williams

CW01280432

NEW HOLLAND

First published in Australia in 2004 by
New Holland Publishers (Australia) Pty Ltd
Sydney • Auckland • London • Cape Town

14 Aquatic Drive Frenchs Forest NSW 2086 Australia
218 Lake Road Northcote Auckland New Zealand
86 Edgware Road London W2 2EA United Kingdom
80 McKenzie Street Cape Town 8001 South Africa

Copyright © 2004 in text: Clive Williams
Copyright © 2004 New Holland Publishers (Australia) Pty Ltd

All rights reserved. No part of this publication may be reproduced, stored in a retrieval system or transmitted, in any form or by any means, electronic, mechanical, photocopying, recording or otherwise, without the prior written permission of the publishers and copyright holders.

National Library of Australia Cataloguing-in-Publication Data:

Williams, Clive, 1945—.
Terrorism explained: the facts about terrorism and terrorist groups.

ISBN 1 74110 084 4.

1. Terrorism—History. 2. Terrorists—History. 3. Terrorism—Economic aspects. 4. Political violence. 5. Terrorism—Prevention. I. Title.

303.625

Project Editor: Liz Hardy
Designer: Karlman Roper
Production Manager: Linda Bottari
Printed in Australia by Griffin Press, Adelaide

10 9 8 7 6 5 4 3 2 1

CONTENTS

PREFACE

I started this book while working at the University of California at San Diego, where I was running a Masters level terrorism program in the first half of 2003. I had long been aware of the lack of a suitable basic text on terrorism and it seemed an opportune time to do something about it.

There was a lull in public interest in terrorism at the time because Operation 'Iraqi Freedom' was receiving saturation media coverage, which also meant that, with the spotlight taken off terrorism, my time was more my own. Unfortunately, this situation changed with the Al Qaeda bombings of Western residential compounds in Riyadh, Saudi Arabia on 12 May 2003 and Al Qaeda affiliate attacks on Jewish and Spanish targets in Morocco on 16 May 2003.

It is only a matter of time before there is another major Muslim extremist terrorist incident in the United States. This seems inevitable given the insensitive way in which many minority Muslim sections of the US population have been treated, the increased Muslim anger against the United States as a result of its international counterterrorism campaign post-September 11, its unqualified support for Israel and the continuing detention of alleged Al Qaeda and Taliban fighters.

At the same time, there are widespread international suspicions, particularly in Muslim-majority countries, about the Bush administration's strategic agenda in the Middle East. More immediately, the US-led invasion of Iraq seems likely to increase popular support for Al Qaeda and raise the prospect of more terrorist attacks, particularly in Europe, the Middle East and Africa.

Clive Williams
January 2004

12 March 2003—he had both political and criminal enemies who wanted to see him dead. The state-manipulated trial process is unlikely to reveal the true facts of the matter.

Terrorism is generally directed against **non-combatants** because they make easier targets, and such attacks are usually more newsworthy than the killing of military personnel.

Military forces, even when on operations, often describe non-military attacks against them as terrorism. Few would deny that an attack on off-duty soldiers, perhaps drinking in a pub, is terrorism. But when terrorists engage soldiers on operations, even when they use vehicle bombs, it is not as clear-cut. The first use of a car bomb by Iraqis during Operation Iraqi Freedom was quickly branded a terrorist act by US officials.

Some observers have labelled the allied bombing of civilian targets in the Second World War as terrorism. But such state action is usually justified on the basis of it being a situation of total war, where the targeted civilian population was an integral part of the enemy war effort, and therefore civilian centres and populations were seen as legitimate targets.

Returning to my definition, there is unlikely to be disagreement that terrorism is **intended to shock and terrify**, usually to cause a polarisation of the population or to undermine the target government. Sometimes it is intended to cause a violent response by government forces that will generally encourage those members of the public who are uncommitted to side with the terrorists. A classic example was the 1997–1999 campaign in Kosovo, where the Kosovo Liberation Army (KLA) attacked the Serbian Police—who then responded brutally against the Kosovars. The Serbian Police actions alienated the uncommitted Kosovars, who then sided with the KLA. The adverse international publicity associated with the Serb brutality eventually drew in NATO, leading to the defeat of the Serbs.

Osama bin Laden was apparently very much taken with the polarisation aspect of terrorism and it might therefore have been one of the strategic intentions of Al Qaeda's September 11 attacks. If it was, George Bush and his advisers played right into Al Qaeda's hands, because US reactions since then have succeeded in alienating many Muslims. As an effective catalyst for causing international upheaval and removal of civil rights, the September 11 attacks probably had no parallel.

The September 11 attacks also imprinted the threat from terrorism on the public psyche; few who witnessed the collapse of the twin towers of the World Trade Center would now be able to view a major disaster without wondering, initially at least, whether terrorists have been responsible. Where Al Qaeda has been less successful is in getting its strategic aims across to non-Muslims; both in articulating clearly what it is trying to achieve and what the West needs to do to get it to stop—if that is an option.

The final element of the terrorism definition—the **strategic outcome** aspect—is important, because it distinguishes low-order street demonstration violence or spontaneous rioting, from high-order violence that is directed towards achieving a longer-term objective. Terrorists, whether they are part of a group, or loners,[2] are usually working towards a longer-term outcome. Ted Kaczynski, the Unabomber, who worked alone for 18 years was, for example, trying to make the United States less dependent on technology.

While most attention is focused on terrorist groups, we should not forget that the state can also be responsible for terrorism, referred to as 'state terrorism'. Indeed, the state, through instruments of the state, has killed far more people in its efforts to stifle political dissent or crush rival groups, than terrorist groups ever have.

The United Nations has tried to avoid the 'state terror' issue, because some UN member states, such as Iraq pre-2003, China and Israel, are clearly guilty of state terrorism. The UN has also stumbled over the issue of 'good' and 'bad' terrorists. While the United States, European Union, and many others condemn any targeting of civilians, the 56-member Organisation of Islamic Conference insists on exempting 'national liberation movements' and 'resistance to foreign occupation'. They have, in particular, Kashmir and the Israeli-Palestinian conflict in mind.

There is currently no agreed UN definition of terrorism. An agreed UN definition could be the linchpin of a comprehensive treaty against terrorism, drawing in all the terrorism-related UN conventions and treaties. This would compel all 189 UN member-states to crack down on terrorists. Such an agreed definition is not in prospect, which allows states to decide for themselves who the real terrorists are. As for President Bush, he confidently calls them as he sees them!

Another category of definition is **state-sponsored terrorism**. This is where the state either actively or passively supports terrorism by a group or an individual. Iraq's support of the Al Aqsa Martyrs Brigade (an offshoot of Fatah, the Palestinian nationalist movement led by Yasser Arafat), responsible for many of the suicide bombings in Israel, is an example of 'active' support. Another is Iran's support for Shiite Hezbollah groups in Saudi Arabia and Lebanon. Passive support is where a state turns a blind eye to known terrorist activities in or from the state. US examples include its non-prevention of the activities from Miami of anti-Castro terrorists, and failure to act against the pre-September 11 fundraising activities of the Provisional IRA on the East Coast of the United States. Some would argue that past US actions, such as its support for the Contra violence against the democratically elected Sandinistas in Nicaragua, and its training of extreme right-wing militias in Central and South America, crosses the line into active support of terrorism.

CHAPTER ONE

THE EARLY HISTORY OF TERRORISM

The first documented examples of terrorism were the activities of the Zealots in Palestine, during 6–73 AD. The Jewish Zealots were attempting to resist Roman rule. It is said that their Sicarii, or knife men, would use the cover of crowds to stab Roman officials. The Zealots were eventually forced to flee to the mountain fortress of Masada where they were besieged by Roman forces. When the Romans finally assaulted the fortress, the defenders committed mass suicide rather than be taken alive by the Romans, and 960 of them died. About six of the less committed managed to survive by hiding in the granaries.

Masada is spiritually important to the Israelis because of the scale of the sacrifice. Oaths of allegiance for Israeli special force units are sometimes taken at Masada for that reason.

Advocates for the legitimacy of terrorism argue that targeting by terrorists of 'forces of occupation', as in the Roman/Zealot situation, is justifiable. A Palestinian academic argued to me that 'just war' theory permits the use of violence against occupation forces and illegal occupiers, such as the Israeli military and Jewish settlers in the West Bank and the Gaza Strip. In his view, Palestinian suicide bombings in Israel proper were not justifiable because he recognised the right of Israel to exist. Palestinian terrorist groups justify such attacks on the basis that they lay claim to the whole of Israel and it has no right to exist at all.

Returning to historical antecedents, the Assassins were active in the Middle East during 1094–1273. They were a sect of Muslim Shiites, founded by Hasan-e Sabbah, who attacked Christians and orthodox Muslim rulers, using suicide tactics. Assassin disciples were apparently exposed to hashish to make them more compliant; the term assassin is said to have originated from the Arabic word for hashish. The Assassins were active in Persia, Iraq and later Syria—until the invading Mongols eventually subdued them. The religious group headed today by the Aga Khan is said to have evolved from the same sect.

An early example of European state terrorism is provided by the activities of the Catholic Church during the Inquisition. Individuals were tortured and executed if they did not conform to Church doctrine. State terrorism was however relatively common in the Middle Ages; invading armies routinely slaughtered civilian populations, particularly if they were in walled cities that had held out for a protracted period against a besieging army. Incidentally, the earliest form of biological warfare was the hurling of diseased corpses into besieged cities to cause disease and weaken the defenders' will to resist. The first recorded instance of this was in 1321.

In 1605, Guy Fawkes and a group of Papist (Roman Catholic) plotters attempted to kill Protestant parliamentarians in Britain by blowing up the Houses of Parliament. A relative of one of the plotters betrayed them. He, a parliamentarian, had been tipped off not to enter Parliament on the day of the planned attack. A search of the premises was conducted and gunpowder found stacked in the basement. Fawkes and the other plotters were arrested. Fawkes was hung, drawn and quartered. The annual English ceremony of burning an effigy of Guy Fawkes on 5 November each year was originally introduced to underline to Catholics that if they stepped out of line, they could share Fawkes's fate. Few who enjoy the burning of the Guy today are aware of its original intent of keeping the Catholics in line!

The French 'terror' during 1793–94 is another example of state terrorism. Mock trials, executions and massacres associated with the French revolution killed an estimated 17,000 people. The word terrorism is said to have come into common usage following the revolution in France.

The Thugs, a secret brotherhood of stranglers and followers of the Hindu goddess Kali, were active throughout India from the 13th century until the mid-1800s. Their existence had long been suspected, but it was the investigative work of a British administrator, Sir William Sleeman, that finally revealed the extent of their activities. 'Thugs' were born into the profession, membership passing from father to son. One Thug leader's confession stated that he led 20–30 men who infested the high road between Agra and Benares. The leader, aged 30, admitted to strangling 100 travellers himself, and to having seen 250 others strangled. His father was a Thug, as was his father before him. The Thugs strangled travellers as a tribute to Kali but were allowed to keep some of the takings for themselves.

In 1866, the Ku Klux Klan (KKK) was formed in the southern part of the United States as a means of keeping the blacks in line after the Civil War had freed them from slavery. Over the next 60 years, the KKK was responsible for extra-judicial killings of blacks, often with official connivance. There were more than 3000 extra-judicial lynchings during this period in the southern United States, many promoted by the KKK. The KKK peaked in membership during the 1920s depression, when there was increased poverty and competition for jobs. The KKK still exists today, with small international chapters, but is an organisation much reduced in influence.

In 1868, Prince Alfred, Duke of Edinburgh, the first royal visitor to Australia, was shot in the back at a picnic at Clontarf Beach in Sydney. The attacker was Henry James O'Farrell, an alleged Fenian, or Irish nationalist, from the adjoining state of Victoria. Prince Alfred survived, but the incident caused much ill feeling between the colonies of New South Wales and Victoria. O'Farrell was a Catholic and it is claimed that the attack also led to the separate Catholic and Protestant schooling systems in Australia. O'Farrell was hung about three weeks after the attack.

From 1883 to 1885 the Fenians mounted a bombing campaign in London that led to the formation of the Irish branch of the Metropolitan Police, later to become the well-known Police Special Branch. Special Branches exist today in many British Commonwealth countries. Their role is to monitor and counter security threats to the state, which in today's world means that their main focus is on the threat from terrorism.

During the latter part of the 19th century and the early part of the 20th century, there was an increase in assassination activity by revolutionaries and anarchists. In the 1880s and 1890s it included the assassination of: Tsar Alexander II of Russia, the Presidents of France and Italy, the Kings of Portugal and Italy, the Prime Minister of Spain and the Empress of Austria. There were also attempts on the German Kaiser and Chancellor. In 1901, an assassin killed President McKinley of the United States. The targets in this period were almost always government officials, rather than civilians.

The most devastating assassination in terms of its immediate consequences was the Serbian Black Hand's assassination in 1914 of the visiting Austrian Archduke Ferdinand at Sarajevo. That one act started a sequence of events that led to the First World War. At least eight million people were to die in that conflict.

During the Boer War of 1899–1902, the Boers were accused by the British of engaging in terrorism because they did not wear uniform and adopted 'unacceptable' tactics, somewhat reminiscent of today's irregular Iraqi attacks in Iraq. Eventually, the Boers and other irregular forces were given recognition and prisoner of war status on the proviso that they openly carried arms, did not disguise their appearance in order to pass as civilians, acted lawfully towards prisoners, and operated under a recognised leader.

During the First World War, Lawrence of Arabia and the Arab armies were accused of terrorism, particularly because of their attacks on civilian trains and the slaughter of civilian passengers. Lawrence justified these actions on the ground that the trains often contained enemy Turkish troops and that, in any case, he himself had no real control over the Arab armies who traditionally gained recruits and were held together by the division of war spoils.

The Bolsheviks used acts of terrorism in the lead-up to successfully seizing power in 1917 in Russia, with the bomb being their favoured weapon. Russian leaders continued thereafter to use terrorism, mainly through staged trials or killings by the state, to consolidate and protect their power. I will return to Stalin later.

During the First World War, the British continued to have terrorism problems in Ireland. Paradoxically, at the same time, Irish units were fighting valiantly as part of the British Army in Europe. The problems in Ireland culminated in Sinn Fein's abortive 1916 Easter rebellion. In 1920, Michael Collins was dispatched by the President of Sinn Fein, Éamon de Valera, to take part in peace talks in London. Collins gained independence for the south, with the north to remain British. It seems likely that de Valera 'set up' Collins. The partition agreement enraged extreme elements of the IRA who saw it as a sell-out, and they ambushed and killed Collins in 1922.

Stalin came to power in Russia in 1924. His leadership brought with it several decades of state terror. His paranoia and economic reforms led to millions of deaths in Russia. Local tribunals tried 'enemies of the state', with a death sentence being the usual outcome. In 1940, Stalin had his outspoken former comrade, Leon Trotsky, who was living in exile in Mexico, murdered. Somewhat surprisingly an ice axe was used; hardly an item that one would expect to be readily available in Mexico. Trotsky's sin was being critical of Stalin's policies. (Expatriates of repressive regimes have often been targeted overseas for highlighting problems back home. They are usually killed by the regime's intelligence service, or by contracted criminals. This is an extension of state terrorism.)

Meanwhile, the problems of the Balkans continued to spill over into Europe, resulting in the assassination of King Alexander I of Yugoslavia in Marseilles in 1934.

Hitler's Germany used state terrorism to purge the country and its occupied territories of Jews, gipsies and Slavs. Hitler regarded them all as sub-human species. The principal state tools for doing this were the Gestapo and the SS. The gipsies have never had a forum to publicise repression of their people but Jews internationally, and the state of Israel itself, have ensured that the world will not forget the cost to its people of Hitler's bizarre ethnic views—or of the continuing dangers from Nazi and anti-Jewish extremism. Holocaust museums now exist in a number of countries.

Mao Tse-tung in China did not use terrorism in the lead up to gaining control of the country in 1949. There were certainly excesses on both sides during the civil war, but probably more so by the nationalists under Chiang Kai-shek than by the communists. Mao had the foresight to seek popular support from the masses for his prospective regime. Mao did however later encourage violence and terrorism against 'counter-revolutionary elements' to consolidate his power and entrench his communist dynasty.

The Second World War and its aftermath saw many insurgent groups in Third World countries use terrorism as part of their campaigns to prevent the colonising powers from re-establishing themselves after the war, or to force them out.

The first substantial success was by the Jews in Palestine. The Jewish nationalist groups Irgun and Lehi (or Stern gang) were responsible for continual terrorist incidents and attacks on the Palestine Police, British Army and British dependants during the 1940s. At the same time, there were well-documented Jewish massacres of Palestinian villagers to free up land for Israeli settlement—what would now be referred to as 'ethnic cleansing'.

The major Jewish terrorist incident was the Irgun bombing of the King David Hotel in Jerusalem in July 1946 that killed 91 people, only 30 of whom were members of the British headquarters that was located in the hotel. The British withdrew in May 1948, and the state of Israel came into being that same month.

Other insurgency and terrorism successes followed in Indonesia, Vietnam, Cyprus, Algeria, Angola, Mozambique and elsewhere. Malaya was one of the few places in Asia where the colonial power prevailed. British Commonwealth forces fought the 'Communist Terrorists' (CTs) during a state of emergency that lasted from 1948 to 1960. Success was eventually achieved through a combination of factors: separation of the CTs from their civilian food suppliers, effective use of psychological warfare (psywar) and amnesty programs, good Special

Branch intelligence, a lack of external logistic support for the CTs, and relentless security force pursuit of the CTs in their jungle hide-outs. The eventual death toll in Malaya was 6711 CTs, 1346 police, 519 soldiers, and 2473 civilians—with another 810 civilians missing.

The Indian independence process led to the partition of India and Pakistan in 1947. Sikhs who had been demanding independence from India for the Sikh state of Khalistan became militant, and conducted acts of terrorism in India. With Sikh emigration to Canada and other countries, Sikh terrorism against Indian targets spread overseas.

In 1947, India also occupied Kashmir—under false pretences according to Pakistan. Several wars have been fought between India and Pakistan over Kashmir, leading to the present Line of Control dividing Pakistani Azad Kashmir from Indian Kashmir. Kashmir is an ongoing cause of Pakistan-backed terrorism into Indian Kashmir, to try to force India to hold a plebiscite on Kashmir's future.

In Kenya, in 1948, the British faced a difficult security situation with the growth of the Kikuyu-led Mau Mau terrorist organisation. The Mau Mau administered blood oaths to its members and conducted secret bonding ceremonies. They attempted to drive British farmers from Kikuyu land by attacking remote homesteads and butchering the occupants to try to terrify other settlers into leaving. At the same time, they intimidated or murdered local natives who were cooperating with the British. They were also reported to have used plant toxins against cattle. The State of Emergency in Kenya lasted from 1952 to 1959 and resulted in the eventual defeat of the Mau Mau. But the British Government's will to remain a colonial power was undermined by the financial cost of dealing with the security problems in many of its colonies. Britain eventually gave Kenya its independence in 1963.

During 1955–59, EOKA terrorists became a major security problem for the British on the Mediterranean island of Cyprus. The EOKA terrorist organisation was fighting for independence from British rule and union with Greece. As in Palestine, there were indiscriminate EOKA terrorist attacks against civilians, particularly against Cypriots locally employed by the British administration. Britain eventually relinquished control of

Cyprus in 1960, but still retains control of two sovereign base areas in the Greek-controlled part of the partitioned island.

Aden, in Yemen, became Britain's next overseas problem area, with National Liberation Front (NLF) terrorism being conducted against the British presence from 1963 to 1967. British forces withdrew in 1967.

In South Africa, the long established African National Congress (ANC) turned to terrorism in 1960 to promote its cause, leading to the arrest and long-term imprisonment of Nelson Mandela, later to become the South African President and highly respected international statesman.

France's colonial problems centred initially on Indochina, where, after a campaign involving insurgency and terrorism, the Viet Minh conventionally defeated the French Army at Dien Bien Phu in 1954. The focus then turned to Algeria, where a bloody insurgent and terrorist campaign was fought from 1954 to 1961. Algeria gained its independence from France in 1962.

In Cuba, Fidel Castro fought against the US-backed Batista regime from 1956 until his forces prevailed in January 1959. Cuba then exported revolutionary ideas and encouraged terrorism in Latin America.

In the 1960s in South and Central America, Raul Sendic founded the Tupamaros in Uruguay, Carlos Marighella founded the National Liberating Alliance in Brazil, while Yon Sosa founded the M-13 Movement in Guatemala. The aim of all of the groups was to work towards a more equitable distribution of national resources. Most of the support for these left-wing movements came from landless or poor peasants who were being exploited by rich landowners. At the same time, the United States supported right-wing dictators, some of whom the United States had put into power as a means of preventing left-wing groups from establishing communist states in its 'backyard'. Cuban support for revolutionary movements declined after Che Guevara was killed in Bolivia in 1967.

CHAPTER TWO

TERRORISM 1968 TO TODAY

Terrorism specialists generally recognise 1968 as a watershed year for terrorism. There were several reasons for this. Most important were the after-effects of the 1967 Six-Day War, during which Israel had comprehensively defeated the attacking armies of Syria, Jordan and Egypt, leaving the Palestinians despairing of ever achieving a Palestinian state through conventional warfare.

Then there was a wave of socialist and anarchist idealism that swept university campuses in western Europe and Japan.

There was also growing opposition internationally, but particularly in the United States, to American involvement in the Vietnam War. This opposition was assisted by improved international air and communications links and better TV coverage, including the arrival of colour TV in the United States, that provided graphic coverage of the Vietnam War and helped to build opposition to the conflict.

And there were stirrings of discontent among those who felt disadvantaged and discriminated against in the United States, Northern Ireland, Spain, and Central and South America. It proved to be a volatile mix.

Many states, particularly communist Russia, East Germany, North Korea, and Cuba, as well as some of the Arab states, saw opportunities for attacking state rivals clandestinely by providing covert support and/or sanctuary to some of the terrorist groups.

Terrorist groups seeking greater autonomy for the populations they 'represented' became active in Northern Ireland, Spain and elsewhere.

Sometimes this bid for greater autonomy included the establishment of 'no-go' areas as a symbol of local control.

European, Japanese and US terrorist groups targeted symbols of national power or capitalism. This resulted in attacks against politicians, diplomats, prominent businesspeople, Jews, capitalist and Western infrastructure and transportation systems.

In 1975, Illich Ramirez Sanchez also known as 'Carlos the Jackal' established the International Front of Revolutionaries, the first ever grouping of like-minded terrorist groups. Terrorist groups cooperated to achieve common objectives, or out of sympathy for each other's cause. Some 700 terrorist groups were active internationally between 1968 and 1972.

Single-issue groups may also turn to violence. These groups focus mainly on right to life, environmental, and animal rights issues, but sometimes attract violent elements.

Other groups that are potentially violent include anarchist elements, often involved in anti-globalisation demonstrations, and cults (which usually have some religious or spiritual basis). Some cults have advocated mass suicide, an example being Jim Jones's group that mass suicided in Guyana, South America in 1978, with 913 members dying.

State-sponsored action

States have been active perpetrators of terrorism in the period from 1968 onwards. In Argentina, the ruling military junta killed 30,000 'leftists' during 1976–83. Many of them were dropped from military aircraft into the Atlantic, where offshore currents took the bound bodies out to sea.

In Chile, thousands disappeared during 1973–90 under the Pinochet regime. International attempts to bring Pinochet to justice have foundered because bringing Pinochet to account has been accorded a lower priority than other national interests. For example, the United Kingdom was reluctant to prosecute Pinochet following his arrest in the

United Kingdom in 1998. He attracted establishment support because of his facilitation of British military operations during the Falklands War. He was allowed to leave the United Kingdom after 16 months, on the ground that he was 'medically unfit to stand trial'.

In Iraq, the 1963 US-supported coup brought the Ba'ath Socialist Party to power. This, in turn, provided the conduit for Saddam Hussein to become responsible for internal security in 1968, and to gain power in 1979. State terror led to tens of thousands of deaths since then. For much of the time until the overthrow of Saddam in April 2003, Iraq supported Palestinian terrorist groups, many of whom maintained offices in Baghdad. When necessary, Palestinian and other Muslim terrorists have been able to obtain medical treatment in Baghdad. There is no evidence however of any active cooperation between Iraq and Al Qaeda.

North Korea has been another perpetrator of State terrorism, but the target in this case was its ideological rival, South Korea. North Korea was active internationally against South Korean interests in the 1980s when it was responsible for a terrorist bombing in Rangoon, Burma, and the downing of a Korean Air jet over the Andaman Sea.

In the Rangoon case, in 1983, North Korean army officers planted bombs in the roof of the Martyrs' Memorial in Rangoon. The remote-controlled explosions killed 21, including 17 members of a South Korean government delegation. The Deputy Prime Minister and three cabinet ministers were killed, but they missed President Chun Doo Hwan.

In 1987, Korean Air flight 858, flying from Baghdad to Bangkok via Abu Dhabi with 115 people on board, disappeared over the Andaman Sea, off Burma. Two North Korean agents, posing as Japanese nationals, placed explosives in an overhead locker and left the flight at Abu Dhabi. They were arrested in Bahrain and took poison. Kim Hyun Hee survived and confessed that she planted a bomb on her government's orders to disrupt the 1987 South Korean elections and the 1988 Seoul Olympics. She stood trial in South Korea, served a jail term, and is now a social worker in South Korea. North Korea is still listed as a state sponsor of terrorism by the United States.

With the end of the Cold War around 1990, most communist support for terrorist groups dried up, creating problems for Marxist and Maoist oriented terrorist groups. The main international problem then became Muslim-extremist groups.

Right-wing extremist groups

Right-wing extremism has been a problem in Western societies since the 1980s, with violent racist groups like **Combat 18**[3] operating in the United Kingdom, and less violent manifestations, such as the **National Front** and the **Australian Nationalist Movement (ANM)** in Australia. Timothy McVeigh, the 1995 Oklahoma bomber, was part of the US right wing, comprising a range of groups including anti-government 'patriots'. In Oklahoma, he seems to have acted mainly with support from Terry Nichols, but possibly with others in the background.

A Jewish right-wing equivalent is **Kach** (meaning thus) and **Kahane Chai** (meaning Kahane lives). Radical American rabbi, Meir Kahane, founded Kach. Kahane was assassinated in New York in November 1990. His son, Binyamin, then formed Kahane Chai. Yigal Amir, who assassinated Israeli Prime Minister Yitzhak Rabin in November 1995, was associated with the group. It aims to recreate the biblical state of Israel. It has been responsible for a number of terrorist attacks on Palestinians. Binyamin and his wife were themselves killed by chance by Palestinians in a drive-by shooting.

Palestinian terrorist groups

The most influential international element in this period was the Palestinian terrorist groups whose activities were mainly intended to focus international attention on the plight of the landless Palestinians. The **Palestine Liberation Organisation (PLO)**, which was formed in 1964, turned to violence in 1967. Ahmed Shukeiri was the first Chairman of the PLO; Yasser Arafat became Chairman in 1969. Arafat's Fatah organisation effectively took control of the PLO and instituted an agenda of violence, aimed at achieving international recognition for the Palestinians. At the time, most Palestinians were languishing in refugee camps with their views largely ignored by the international community, including many Arab states. The Palestinians soon turned to high-profile attacks against Western infrastructure with support from both Arab sympathisers and leftist groups.

Fatah as an umbrella organisation included Black September, Force 17, the Popular Front for the Liberation of Palestine (PFLP), the PFLP-GC (GC for General Command), the Democratic Front for the Liberation of Palestine (DFLP), also known as the Peoples' Democratic Front for the Liberation of Palestine (PDFLP, Hawatmeh faction), as well as the Al Aqsa Martyrs Brigade. (The PLO and Fatah renounced violence in 1993 following the Oslo Accords.) The Palestinian groups continually fluctuated in size and significance as fighters transferred their allegiance to follow the most successful leader.

Black September also known as the **Abu Nidal Organisation (ANO)** was, and is, a typical PLO splinter group. It was responsible for a number of major attacks in the 1970s and 1980s, including the Munich Olympics attack in 1972 and the Rome and Vienna airport attacks in 1985. It was mainly based in Libya, which made defection of its members to other groups more difficult. Abu Nidal, the leader of the group was paranoid about loyalty and would have those whose loyalty he doubted, buried in the sand with a tube from their mouth to the surface, while he pondered their fate. Some he dug up alive, some were shot down the tube, others he left buried to die.

The **PFLP-GC** was another PLO splinter group, led by Ahmad Jibril, based in Lebanon; it has been largely dormant since 1987, but is suspected of involvement in the Lockerbie bombing in 1988. It is probable that Libyan agents *were* involved in the actual bombing, but it seems likely that they were working for the PFLP-GC. There is compelling evidence that the PFLP-GC was contracted to do the attack by the Iranians; the motive being revenge for the downing of an Iranian Airbus passenger aircraft by the USS Vincennes in July 1988. Pan Am flight 103 was supposed to have been downed over the Atlantic to destroy the evidence, but a flight delay meant that it was destroyed over Scotland instead.

The **Palestinian Islamic Jihad (PIJ)** was formed in the 1970s in the Gaza Strip and aims for the destruction of Israel and the creation of an Islamic Palestinian state. It has been responsible for many suicide bombings in Israel and is still active. (There are many 'Islamic jihad' groups so they are often distinguished in Western reporting by placing the country of origin first in the title.)

The Palestinian **15 May Organisation** was formed in 1979, and was responsible for a number of international attacks, including in Australia, before it was absorbed back into Fatah, which renounced international violence in 1993.

The **Palestinian Islamic Resistance Movement**, commonly known as **Hamas**, was formed in 1987, mainly as a social support organisation, but with radical fringe elements. Its spiritual leader was Sheikh Ahmed Yassin. (Yassin had been imprisoned by the Israelis but was released as part of a deal following a botched Mossad assassination attempt in Jordan against Khaled Meshal, one of Hamas' political leaders. He was assassinated by Israeli forces in March 2004.) Hamas seeks to replace Israel with a Palestinian state and draws its main support from the West Bank. It has been responsible for a large number of attacks on Israel.

Europe and the United States

Other violent groups in the 1960s and 1970s included the **Angry Brigade** in the United Kingdom, and the **Weather Underground** and **Black Panthers** in the United States.

The **Angry Brigade** was a loose group of British 'new left' anarchists in the early-1970s who planted bombs, but failed to build any significant level of support amongst the British working class. They were crushed as soon as the state turned its attention to them. In a major trial of eight people at the Old Bailey, four of the accused were sentenced to ten years each for conspiracy, while four were acquitted. The Angry Brigade's fight against international capital saw them explode over a hundred bombs without killing anyone, and they were eclipsed by the arrival of violent PIRA terrorism, which targeted civilians and became much more of a security concern.

The American **Weather Underground** was a terrorist faction of the Students for a Democratic Society. In 1970, one of its leaders, Bill Ayers was said to have summed up the Weatherman philosophy as: 'Kill all the rich people. Break up their cars and apartments. Bring the revolution home, kill your parents, that's where it's really at.' Between 1970 and 1974 they were responsible for at least 12 bombings. Arrests and a bomb accident took its toll on the members, and by the mid-1980s, the Weather Underground was essentially history.

The **Black Panther Party for Self-Defense** was an American black revolutionary party founded in 1966 in Oakland, California, by Huey Newton and Bobby Seale. The party's original purpose was to patrol black ghettoes 'to protect residents from acts of police brutality'. The Panthers eventually developed into a Marxist revolutionary group that called for the arming of all blacks, the exemption of blacks from the draft and from all sanctions of so-called white America, the release of all blacks from jail, and the payment of compensation to blacks for centuries of exploitation by white Americans. At its peak in the late 1960s, Panther membership exceeded 2000 and the organisation operated chapters in several major cities. Conflicts between Black Panthers and police in the late 1960s and early 1970s led to shoot-outs in California, New York, and Chicago, one of which resulted in Newton's going to prison for the murder of a police patrolman. By the mid-1970s, having lost many members and having fallen out of favour with many American black leaders, who objected to the party's methods, the Panthers turned from violence to concentrate on conventional politics and on providing social services in black neighbourhoods. The party was effectively disbanded by the early 1980s.

In western Europe the leading group from 1968 was the **Baader-Meinhof Group** (named after the founders, Andreas Baader and Ulrike Meinhof), later to become known as the Red Army Faction. Its aim was to destroy Western capitalism through terrorism, and thereby help precipitate a worldwide Marxist revolution. It also tried to undermine German–US solidarity, and used violence to pressure the authorities to release imprisoned members. Its main activities were assassinations and kidnappings of prominent German and US officials, and bombings—mainly of US military targets. The group probably never exceeded more than 20–30 hard-core members, but had several hundred sympathisers. The core members were able to lie low in East Germany when things became too hot for them elsewhere in Europe.

The Red Brigades was founded by Renato Curcio in Italy in 1969. It had less than 100 hard-core members but was responsible for a number of high profile attacks, including the kidnapping and murder of former Italian Prime Minister Aldo Moro in 1978, and the kidnapping of US General Dozier in 1981. Dozier was later rescued by the Italian police. The aims of the Red Brigades were to destroy the Italian government through revolutionary action, attack NATO targets in Italy, and destroy 'imperialist multinational corporations'. The Red Brigades is still active today as the Red Brigades for the Construction of a Combatant Communist Party (BR-PCC), but has only a small membership.

The Provisional Irish Republican Army also known as **PIRA**, or the **Provos**, was established by militant Catholics in Belfast in 1969, with a political wing, Sinn Fein. Younger Catholic militants were concerned that the Irish Liberation Army (IRA) leaders were old and soft and no longer motivated to fight for Catholic rights. PIRA's immediate objective was to provide backing in Northern Ireland for the minority Catholic population against violent Protestant elements. At its height, it had several hundred members and thousands of sympathisers among the Catholic population. Its support declined as supporters wearied of the violence. PIRA also became less relevant as the British and Northern Ireland governments addressed many of the sectarian grievances, such as discrimination in employment, and the lack of Catholic representation in the police force of Northern Ireland.

European groups, such as PIRA and the Red Army Faction, and the Palestinian groups, as well as the Japanese Red Army, formed cooperative links through common training in Lebanon's Bekaa Valley.

Central and South America

In Peru, in the late 1960s, former university professor, Abimael Guzman, formed **Sendero Luminoso** (**Shining Path** or **SL**), and his teachings created the foundation of SL's militant Maoist doctrine. In the 1980s, SL became one of the most ruthless terrorist groups in the Western Hemisphere—approximately 30,000 people have died since Shining Path took up arms in 1980. Its stated goal is to destroy existing Peruvian institutions and replace them with a communist peasant revolutionary regime. It also opposes any influence by foreign governments, as well as by other Latin American guerrilla groups, especially the rival Peruvian **Tupac Amaru Revolutionary Movement (MRTA)**, which was formed in 1983. Abimael Guzman was captured in 1992 and since then his organisation has been in decline.

The Indian subcontinent, Asia and the South Pacific

In Sri Lanka, the **Liberation Tigers of Tamil Eelam (LTTE)**, also known as the **Tamil Tigers**, was established in 1976 to fight for an independent Tamil state. The LTTE has some 10,000 combatants. It fights conventionally but also uses terrorist suicide attacks to target government officials and the Singhalese population. Some 50,000 Indian troops were deployed to Sri Lanka as peacekeepers in 1987–88 to monitor a cease-fire. The cease-fire broke down and the Indian troops ended up siding with the Sri Lankan government forces until heavy casualties caused them to withdraw in 1990. So far there have been an estimated 64,000 deaths in the Sri Lankan civil war. Currently, a Norway-brokered cease-fire is in place.

In the Philippines, the Maoist **New People's Army (NPA)** was formed in 1969 as the military wing of the Communist Party of the Philippines (CPP). It was mainly rural-based but had city-based assassination squads known as Sparrow Units. It has been in decline since 1990, in part due to the collapse of communism.

Filipino Abdurajak Abubakar Janjalani formed the Philippines **Abu Sayyaf Group (ASG)** in 1991, as a breakaway group from the Moro National Liberation Front (MNLF). Janjalani had been a Mujaheddin fighter in Afghanistan; whether he had contact with Osama bin Laden, as claimed, is not known, but the jihad experience encouraged him to form a breakaway terrorist group in the southern Philippines on his return. The ASG under Abdurajak Abubakar Janjalani sought a fundamentalist state in Mindanao and the Sulu Archipelago. It has been responsible for a number of attacks on Catholic Filipinos and has captured foreigners for ransom, some of whom it has beheaded. Since Janjalani's death in 1998, it has degenerated into being largely a criminal group, colluding at times with local officials and the Armed Forces of the Philippines. The latter's interest has been to obtain part of the ransom money generated by ASG's activities. The group is now broken up into at least three factions.

The **Japanese Red Army (JRA)** was formed in 1970. It only had about 15 members, but aimed to foster world revolution in cooperation with other groups. It was responsible for a number of bloody attacks, including at Tel Aviv's Lod Airport in 1972, where three JRA operatives killed 26 people, mainly Ethiopian Christians, for the Palestinian cause. The JRA was later based in Lebanon. Some members have been given sanctuary in North Korea, but most of its members are now in jail in Japan.

Shoko Asahara formed the **Aum Shinrikyo (Aum Supreme Truth)** millenarian cult in Japan in 1987. It aimed to bring about 'World War III' and a situation of Armageddon. It developed a substantial overseas following, particularly in Russia. It was responsible for, among other acts of violence, the Tokyo sarin gas attack in 1995. Japan banned Aum Shinrikyo in 1995, but it is still active in Japan as Aleph. Many of the Aum Shinrikyo members released from jail since 1995 have joined Aleph.

In Cambodia, the communist **Khmer Rouge (KR)** came to power in the late 1970s. They used extreme, violent methods in their attempt to create a classless agrarian utopia and were responsible for the Cambodian genocide under Pol Pot in the late 1970s, and for killing a number of Westerners. The KR is now largely defunct, but many of the former middle ranking KR are serving in the Cambodian Government (including Prime Minister Hun Sen).

The Indonesian annexation of East Timor in 1976 led to the creation of **Fretilin** (Revolutionary Force for an Independent East Timor), with its military wing Falintil. The group was mainly involved in fighting the Indonesian military but the Indonesian military was itself responsible for a large number of well-documented acts of terrorism. Australia, which was concerned about the possibility of having another Cuba on its doorstep, acquiesced to the 1976 Indonesian takeover, and subsequently turned a blind eye to Indonesian excesses—despite official knowledge of what was happening.[4]

Another separatist group, the **Free Papua Movement (OPM)** has been in existence since 1963. Its most noteworthy act was the kidnapping of seven foreigners in Indonesian Irian Jaya (now West Papua) in 1996. Indonesian Special Forces freed them. The OPM has also been blamed by Indonesian officials for incidents such as the Freeport mine shooting of Americans in West Papua in August 2002. Suspicion for the attack fell initially on the OPM, but Elsham (the leading human rights group in Indonesian Papua), says that the Indonesian security force protecting the mine may have carried out the attack.

The OPM has been largely inactive in recent years, although it shows signs of resurgence in West Papua where it claims to protect native rights against the Indonesian occupiers.

Eastern Europe, the Middle East and North Africa

The **Kurdistan Workers' Party (PKK)** was formed in 1974, mainly comprising Turkish Kurds. It aimed to create an independent Kurdish state. The PKK sees the hard-line anti-Kurdish policies of the Turkish Government as the main impediment to achieving an autonomous Kurdish state in an area comprising parts of Turkey, Iraq and Iran. The PKK's main target has been the Turkish government, both in Turkey and abroad. It has been less active since the capture by Turkish Special Forces of its leader Abdullah Ocalan in February 1999 in Nairobi, Kenya, and the establishment of a de facto Kurdish state in northern Iraq since the 1991 Gulf War.

The **Justice Commandos of the Armenian Genocide (JCAG)** was formed in 1975 with the same aim as the PKK—to establish an independent state, in its case, for Armenians. It also sought revenge against Turkey for the Armenian genocides. JCAG attacks against Turkish officials took place internationally, including in Sydney and Melbourne, Australia. JCAG is no longer active because Armenia gained independent statehood with the break-up of the former Soviet Union.

In Egypt, two terrorist groups were formed in the 1970s, the **al-Jihad** also known as the **Egyptian Islamic Jihad** (EIJ), and **al-Gama'a al-Islamiyya** (the **Islamic Group** or **IG**). The EIJ has concentrated on killing Egyptian officials to try to overthrow the state (including the assassination of Anwar Sadat in 1981), while the IG has tried to undermine the Egyptian government by attacking police and tourists (inlcuding the 1997 attack in Luxor that killed 58 tourists). Some leading Egyptian extremists, who had sought sanctuary in Albania, were arrested when Albania became ungovernable and were returned covertly by the CIA to Egypt for trial.

Both groups are currently in decline, although many members of EIJ are now active with Al Qaeda, including Dr Ayman al-Zawahiri, who has become Al Qaeda's deputy leader. IG's spiritual leader is Sheikh

Omar Abdul Rahman, who was resettled in the US by the CIA as a reward for his activities in the Afghan war against the Russians in the 1980s. Somewhat naively, the CIA seemed to believe that 'the enemy of my enemy is my friend'. Rahman was convicted in 1995 of seditious conspiracy, bombing conspiracy, soliciting an attack on a US military installation, and soliciting the murder of Egyptian President Hosni Mubarak. His followers were also indicted for plotting to bomb bridges, tunnels and landmarks in New York for which Rahman allegedly had given his blessing.

The Marxist **Revolutionary People's Liberation Party/Front** (DHKP/C), better known as **Devrimci Sol**, or **Dev Sol**, was formed in Turkey in 1978. Dev Sol was a splinter faction of Dev Genc (Revolutionary Youth). It was renamed DHKP/C in 1994 after factional infighting; 'Party' refers to the group's political activities, while 'Front' is a reference to the group's militant operations. The group espouses a Marxist-Leninist ideology and is virulently anti-US, anti-NATO, and anti-Turkish establishment. It finances its activities chiefly through armed robberies and extortion. It operates only in Turkey, and mainly in Istanbul.

The Iranian revolution, and seizure of the US embassy staff in 1979, signalled a new polarisation of Shiah opposition to the West, and the arrival of a major state sponsor for terrorist attacks against Israeli and US interests.

The **Lebanese Hezbollah**, formed in 1983, was a major beneficiary of this development. Lebanese 'Hezbollah' (there are several 'Hezbollah' groups so, as with 'Islamic jihad', a country prefix is usually used) seeks an Iranian style fundamentalist state in Lebanon. Lebanese Hezbollah was responsible for the US Marine barrack and French military headquarters bombings in Beirut in 1983, the bombing of the US embassy in Beirut in 1984, kidnappings of Westerners in Beirut in the late 1980s, and bombings of Israeli and Jewish facilities in Buenos Aires in 1992 and 1994. Increasingly professional Lebanese Hezbollah insurgent operations drove Israel to withdraw its troops from Israeli-occupied South Lebanon in May 2000.

Osama bin Laden established **Al Qaeda** in 1989. The end of the anti-Soviet war in Afghanistan in 1988 gave him the opportunity to work towards a community of Islamic states stretching from Mindanao to Morocco, using the contacts he developed during the war. Al Qaeda has been very successful in facilitating Muslim extremist attacks against 'unsatisfactory' Muslim rulers and those who oppress or oppose Muslims. In 1998, Osama bin Laden created an 'Islamic Front for Jihad Against the Jews and Crusaders'. Al Qaeda's most successful attacks to date have been the September 11 attacks in the United States.

In retaliation for September 11, the United States mounted Operation Enduring Freedom in October 2001 to destroy Al Qaeda and its sponsor, the Taliban. By the end of 2001, the United States had displaced Al Qaeda from Afghanistan and toppled the Taliban regime. Al Qaeda dispersed mainly to Pakistan and Yemen. In Pakistan, it integrated into the camps of affiliated Muslim extremist groups. It is slowly re-establishing itself in the border areas of Afghanistan, Iran and Pakistan. Because of arrests of about a third of its senior operatives, it is currently more reliant on regional affiliates to conduct activities on its behalf.

Algerian terrorism began in 1992 following the Algerian Government's voiding of an election result that favoured the **Islamic Salvation Front (FIS)**. There are now several Algerian terrorist groups, the best known being the **Armed Islamic Group (GIA)**. The **Salafist Group for Call and Combat (GSPC)** has eclipsed it in influence in recent years. The fighting in Algeria, and the activities of displaced Algerian terrorists in France, have cost more than 100,000 lives.

CHAPTER THREE

TERRORIST MOTIVATIONS

Understanding the motivations of terrorist individuals and terrorist groups is important because it helps us to understand why terrorists are doing what they are doing, their modus operandi, and whether they are prepared to die for the cause (particularly relevant in a siege hostage or hijack situation). Intelligence analysts tend to be focussed more on what is likely to happen in coming days or weeks, rather than the longer term or causative factors. But the latter factors are important to eventual resolution of a terrorism problem.

Regrettably, few operatives have become academics, but one who did so, very successfully, was Major-General Richard Clutterbuck of the British Army. He was a military expert on terrorism before he became an academic at Exeter University, and wrote a number of insightful books on counterterrorism issues.[5]

Former US Defense Intelligence Agency (DIA) analyst, Mark Kauppi has produced some good analysis of terrorism and the motivations of terrorists. In 2000, Kauppi suggested that there were three key motivations for an individual to commit terrorism or become a terrorist.[6] These were ideological, psychological and environmental.

Kauppi noted that ideological factors have always been important to provide a legitimising basis for terrorist violence. He noted the importance of Marxist Leninism for left-wing groups, the works of Mikhail Bakunin for anarchists, and ethnonationalist beliefs for separatist groups or those seeking national independence from colonial powers.[7] Kauppi observed that ideology can become a means to justify and perpetuate the actions of a group and there is a danger of ideologically motivated groups losing sight of what they want to achieve.

Kauppi noted that there is a tendency, particularly on the part of psychologists and psychiatrists, to perceive terrorists as mentally disturbed individuals—termed the 'dispositional' approach. Most researchers agree though that terrorists are essentially rational actors with few of the attributes of the clinically abnormal.

Kauppi stated that to dismiss terrorists as mentally ill or suffering from childhood neuroses is simply wrong. A desire for adventure, a lack of alternatives, and enhancement of self-esteem are all likely to be motivating factors for an individual to become a terrorist. While Kauppi does not address the influence of leaders, an inspirational or charismatic terrorist leader will always be an important recruitment factor. In some contexts, particularly with the Palestinians, where there are many different groups and factions, members tend to be drawn to the most attractive and dynamic leaders. Hence the Israeli policy of targeted killing of such individuals.

Kauppi claimed that the environmental motivations for an individual to commit terrorist acts fall into two categories—grievances and cultures of violence.

Grievances that affect a community can be social, political or economic in nature. A community can be broadly defined, referring for example both to exploited peasants and disadvantaged ethnic or religious groups. Grievances may be longstanding, such as those of the minority Roman Catholics in Northern Ireland or the majority Shiites in Iraq.

Cultures of violence refers to communities that have experienced high levels of violence for many years, so that violence, rather than peace, has become the norm. The situation with the Palestinians in the occupied territories is an example of a culture of violence.

In terms of the individual, the search for a single factor to explain why individuals turn to terrorism is self-defeating, says Kauppi—as with other human behaviour, multiple factors come into play.

Michael Vatikiotis notes that political and economic discontent will increase the number of militants, but that individual extremists are more closely linked to the pursuit of domestic political goals than, say, the desire to join an Islamic empire.[8]

The motivation of the suicide bomber is an area of particular interest, given the popular perception of an increased threat of suicide attacks. There is probably no single psychological or demographic factor that determines the motivation of the suicide bomber.[9] Martyrdom and promises of free entry to heaven for the suicide bomber and family members form part of the equation, but are not the whole story. Female suicide bombers, both Muslim and Hindu Tamil, are more likely to be driven by nationalist ideals. Patriotism, hatred of the enemy, and an intense sense of victimisation—fuelled by lack of alternatives—would seem to be key motivators for suicide bombers.

Kauppi goes on to look at group motivations. He noted that all groups experience a common phenomenon of deindividuation—or increased identification with the actions of the group. Societal non-conformists become group conformists. The process may be achieved through religious study, studies of history, or group discussion. Actions of the group that result in unexpected civilian casualties can be rationalised in the name of the cause and through reduced individual responsibility. All members of the terrorist organisation have a common interest in group survival. Kauppi believes that recruits see membership as a means to an end, while longer-term members probably see terrorism as a lifestyle option.

Kauppi concluded that terrorist motivation is a process that occurs over time; like travelling down a road where you have to decide every so often which fork to take. There is therefore an element of chance in the process.

Martha Crenshaw[10] observed that group dynamics help to explain why a group continues to exist, even after the world around it has profoundly changed. Thus we see Loyalist and Catholic terrorists, who were the fighters for their organisations in Northern Ireland, turning to organised street crime as a group. Or the members of a left-wing group, like the New People's Army in the Philippines, turning to protection rackets in the geographic areas they control, despite the collapse of their ideological (communist) motivation.

CHAPTER FOUR

REGIONAL TERRORISM

International terrorism is defined by the US State Department as 'terrorism involving citizens or the territory of more than one country'.[11] The US State Department data, which is collated each year by the Counterterrorism Center at Langley, Virginia, provides a basis for comparison of international data since about 1980, but it does not include much of the world's terrorism. 'International' terrorism as defined by the State Department probably accounts for no more than 10% of terrorism internationally. 'National' or 'domestic' terrorism, where only one nationality and country is involved, accounts for the remainder of incidents, much of which involves separatist or ethno-nationalist terrorism.

There is no realistic way of accounting for domestic incidents because of bureaucratic cover-ups, failure to maintain local statistics, lack of reporting, and confusion over who might have been responsible for an incident—and why they did it.

In the Philippines, for example, many bombings are related to non-payment of protection money to criminals or corrupt officials. For various reasons, regional governors often do not tell Manila about the state of lawlessness in their areas. It is therefore difficult to ascertain whether an incident is politically or criminally motivated. In China, the authorities usually say that perpetrators of explosive incidents were stressed due to work or personal reasons, rather than acknowledge that an incident was politically motivated. The government approach in China is to cover up or spin what it does not want people to know.

The United States maintains a list of designated regional terrorist organisations. In April 2003 there were 36 on the list. They are listed at Appendix A along with the US list of 'other' terrorist groups.[12]

The United States has also designated a number of regional countries as state sponsors of terrorism. State sponsorship is defined by the United

States as 'the employment of outside individuals or groups by a state, to pursue its policy aims through terrorist methods'.[13] The countries on the US list are: Cuba, Iraq, Iran, Libya, North Korea, Sudan, and Syria. The list does not include two of the worst offenders, Saudi Arabia and Pakistan. The US list is clearly subjective since some of the states on the list have not actively supported terrorism for many years (Cuba, Libya, and North Korea), while others (such as the worst offenders) are left off because they are US allies.

Africa

In Africa, the high level of both politically and criminally motivated violence is mainly tribal or ethnic-based, aggravated by colonial boundaries, poverty, environmental degradation, and un-met social and economic expectations. On a map, comparison of colonial political boundaries with actual tribal boundaries shows why violence is endemic. In many cases, a minority of a tribe will be in one state, where it will be victimised by a majority from a rival tribe. Every so often, the victimisation will become violent, causing a refugee problem and ultimately a backlash from the minority group assisted by other members of their ethnic group from across the border.

Some areas of Africa fare worse than others. The Congo area has a bloody history contributed to by the excesses of the colonial power (Belgium) and its failure to leave the country with an effective administrative structure. Former Portuguese colonies have suffered for similar reasons. Rapacious local rulers, like Zimbabwe's Doctor Mugabe, have also contributed to Africa's poor human rights record.

The Indian subcontinent

In South Asia (the Indian subcontinent), violence is mainly religion-based and/or separatist motivated. Muslims form about 10% of the

Indian population and violence between Muslims and Hindus is common. There are nearly as many Muslims in India as there are in Pakistan (120 million). Muslims ruled India for several hundred years and in the process destroyed Hindu temples and built mosques on the sites. Now that Hindus are in control, the wheel has turned. The destruction of one such mosque to rebuild a temple, at Ayodhya, has resulted in large-scale religiously motivated violence.

Socially based violence is also common in India. In many parts of India, as noted earlier, the subjugation of rural workers (who work for low wages and are continually in debt to the landlord) means that they are practically slaves. Every so often, there are uprisings against landlords and these are violently suppressed. Another aspect is the caste system. Mahatma Gandhi tried to do away with it, but there is still much caste-related violence in India. Sometimes this occurs when lower caste persons are seen to have aspirations 'above their station' or want more than 'their entitlement'.

Regions of India that do not want to be part of India, such as the states known as the 'Seven Sisters' north and east of Bangladesh, present an ongoing security problem for India. India's neighbour, Bangladesh, has a high level of lawlessness and is a haven for wanted terrorists. Elsewhere in India, the Punjab has traditionally been a restless area.

Afghanistan has been, and still is, a sanctuary for Al Qaeda, even though its former sponsor, the Taliban, has been displaced from power.

Pakistan and, to a much lesser extent, India, support terrorism in each other's territory. Pakistan initiates most of the bilateral violence in and through the region of Kashmir. Pakistan supports a number of militant extremist organisations, such as Harakat ul-Mujahidin, Jaish-e-Mohammed and Lashkar-e-Tayyiba, with the aim of eventually forcing India to hold a plebiscite over Kashmir's future. These same organisations assist Al Qaeda and are part of its regional jihad. Many of the Al Qaeda fighters who left Afghanistan are embedded in these groups as an interim arrangement until Al Qaeda can become fully operational again.

In Nepal, a Maoist movement has gained control of large areas of the country and is now capable of mounting large-scale attacks on government forces.

In Sri Lanka, as previously mentioned, the LTTE or Tamil Tigers is probably the best-organised insurgent and terrorist group in Asia. It has fought an insurgency campaign in areas peripheral to those it controls, but has also tried to undermine public support for the Sri Lankan government through terrorist attacks elsewhere in the country. It is currently in ceasefire mode but continues to train and prepare for a return to violence if the Norway-brokered peace process does not deliver acceptable outcomes.

East and South-East Asia

In East Asia, terrorist violence is mainly in support of separatist aspirations. Muslim benefactors support Muslim separatist groups to some extent through charitable donations that find their way to insurgent/terrorist groups, such as the Moro Islamic Liberation Front (MILF) in Mindanao in the Philippines. All of the Muslim extremist groups in East Asia are either engaged in trying to form a separate state or are attacking non-Muslims in the areas in which they operate.

A significant newcomer to the scene since about 1992 is Jemaah Islamiah (JI), a South-East Asian regional group with elements in Singapore, Malaysia, Indonesia, southern Thailand and the southern Philippines. Recent reports also suggested some activity in Cambodia and Burma, but government action in these two countries appears to have prevented any significant problem from developing.

The existence of JI was only discovered after September 11. It is closely affiliated with Al Qaeda and had planned to conduct attacks against US and Western interests in Singapore once given the green light by Al Qaeda. JI's Indonesian element was responsible for the Bali suicide bombings on 12 October 2002, which killed 202 people including 88 Australians, 22 UK nationals and seven Americans (as well as 36 Indonesians and other foreign nationals). It was also responsible for the suicide bombing at the Marriott Hotel in Jakarta on 5 August 2003.

Communism is in general decline in Asia. The only communist insurgent/terrorist group in the region is the New People's Army (NPA) in the Philippines, but it is mainly engaged in criminal activity in the areas that it still controls.

There is some cult activity in East Asia but it is low level. The Japanese group, Aum Shinrikyo, was responsible for the 1995 sarin gas attacks in Tokyo, but the principals were all rounded up. It is now going through a slow rebuild as some of its middle-ranking leaders are released from jail. It has renamed itself Aleph because Aum Shinrikyo has been a banned organisation in Japan since 1995.

Eurasia

In Eurasia, the terrorist violence is mainly separatist-related. Much of the violence has been encouraged by the break-up of the Soviet Union. China's encouragement of of Han Chinese transmigration to Xinjiang, and subsequent marginalisation of the former majority group, the Uigurs, has led to terrorist attacks by the Uigurs. China will not back off because of its need to develop alternative energy sources in Xinjiang. Because the Uigurs are Muslims they have in the past been able to secure assistance from external Muslim terrorist groups, particularly Al Qaeda. Now China is using that link against them and claims that its suppression of the Uigurs is part of the global war on terror.

Russia's ongoing war in Chechnya has led to widespread human rights abuses by Russian forces. The Chechens have retaliated with continued terrorist attacks against Russian civilians. There are suspicions that some of these may have been perpetrated by Russian security forces to allow President Putin to show strong leadership and consolidate his hold on power.

Latin America

In Latin America, much of the violence flows from inequitable distribution of national resources. The United States has traditionally backed right-wing governments and dictators, while left-wing groups have championed the peasants. Both governments and leftist groups have engaged in terrorism in the past. Another dimension is right-wing militias (often funded by governments, and sometimes covertly trained and supported by the United States), who have been responsible for some of the worst excesses. An example is the Colombian United Self Defence Force (AUC)—reportedly funded in the past by the CIA. The United States now lists the AUC as a terrorist organisation because of its massacres of civilians and links with narcotics trafficking.

There are occasional claims that terrorist groups (such as Lebanese Hezbollah) and criminal groups are using the tri-border area of Paraguay, Argentina and Brazil. While criminal groups might be exploiting jurisdictional weaknesses, compelling evidence of terrorist activity there is lacking.

The Middle East

In the Middle East, violence flows mainly from Muslim extremists seeking to gain control of Muslim states.

Meanwhile, Israel's continuing occupation of Palestinian land in the West Bank and the Gaza Strip, Arafat's unpreparedness to compromise and the lack of US will to pressure both towards an equitable peace agreement, are a major cause of ongoing violence. Since signing the Oslo Accords in 1993, Israel has done little to prevent the building of more than 40,000 settler houses in the West Bank and the Gaza Strip. Palestinian suicide attacks against Israel reflect frustration and desperation on the part of the Palestinians at their inability to prevent de facto absorption of their land into greater Israel.

North America

We have seen continued interest since the September 11 attacks in the targeting of Americans in the United States by Al Qaeda and Al Qaeda-affiliated groups (such as the Algerian Armed Islamic Group (GIA)) and individual Muslim sympathisers, mainly because of the United States' Middle East policies and support for Israel. There have been no significant Muslim-extremist attacks in the United States since September 11.

It seems increasingly likely that the crash of Egypt Air Flight 990 in October 1999 was suicide by the Egyptian pilot. It is not clear what his motivation might have been.

The United States also faces internal threats from extreme right-wing and single-issue groups. For example, Timothy McVeigh, the main perpetrator of the 1995 Oklahoma City bombing was believed to be associated with extreme right-wing organisations.

Violent single-issue groups in the US focus mainly on environmental, animal rights and anti-abortion issues.

External threats to US interests from Muslim extremists are also significant. The US-led invasion of Iraq is likely to lead to more Muslim extremist violence against US interests overseas in the future.

Oceania

In Oceania (the South Pacific), there is politically motivated violence in Papua New Guinea and the Solomons, and, in the past, there have been problems in Fiji and New Caledonia. The lawlessness and ethnic problems in PNG and the Solomons will probably continue as both are failing states with little capacity to deal with their internal security problems.

Europe

In Western Europe, there is increasing violence by extreme right-wing and anarchist groups. One extreme right-wing group is the Italian New Red Brigades, a modern offshoot of the Red Brigades that was active in the 1970s. It is opposed to Italy's foreign and labour policies and NATO.

More generally, right-wing extremist and Nazi groups in Europe are opposed to immigrants and coloured people and undertake hate attacks. Anarchism has also grown in popularity and influence as part of the anti-war, anti-capitalist and anti-globalisation movements. Recently, anarchists have been known for their involvement in protests against World Trade Organisation and Group of Seven meetings and the World Economic Forum, protests which are often portrayed in the media as violent riots. Many anarchists were part of the so-called 'black blocs' at these protests and some engaged in rioting, vandalism and violent confrontation with police. There is also ongoing separatist violence in Spain and parts of the Balkans.

Politically motivated violent groups operating outside Europe have long used Europe as a sanctuary, which has meant that they have been reluctant to draw attention to themselves by operating in Europe. Since September 11 authorities have focused more attention on these groups, and a number of terrorist attacks have been thwarted by security authorities.

CHAPTER FIVE

TERRORIST MODUS OPERANDI

The US State Department defines a terrorist group as any group practising, or that has significant subgroups that practise, terrorism. (A group being two or more persons.)

Characteristics of terrorist groups

Some characteristics of a terrorist group are that:

- they are often made up of small cells (five or fewer persons)
- the members are well known to each other
- they are very committed—sometimes prepared to die for their cause
- members are usually well educated or indoctrinated
- their operations are planned thoroughly
- they are well armed and resourced
- members are alert to danger—therefore security conscious
- the group is up-to-date technologically
- the group uses support elements to prepare for operations, and, of course
- their actions are directed towards a longer term objective.

Criteria for successful terrorist action

There are necessary criteria for the operations of terrorist groups to be successful, for example:

- the target has to have symbolic or newsworthy value
- the group needs good prior intelligence—including from reconnaissance and observation
- a support infrastructure is in place
- comprehensive preparation and planning has been undertaken
- all participants are familiar with weapons and explosives, and what they have to do
- preparations have been made for possible glitches or difficulties
- the exit strategy (if it is not a suicide operation) has been determined and safe havens selected, and finally
- the enemy's response has been anticipated for exploitation.

Breakdown of terrorist attacks

The United States' Counterterrorism Center (CTC) recorded 199 terrorist attacks in 2002. These included 137 bombings, 50 armed attacks, five kidnappings, two firebombings, two barricade or hostage situations, one hijack, one assault, and one other. If you aggregate bombings and firebombings each year, you find that bombings normally account for 65–75% of all international incidents. In 2001, the CTC listed the attacks on the World Trade Center and Pentagon as bombings because of the use of the aircraft as fully fuelled 'bombs'.

There have been two other known instances when terrorists planned to use passenger aircraft as weapons. In December 1994, Algerian Armed Islamic Group (GIA) terrorists hijacked an Air France Airbus at Algiers with the intent (according to French authorities) of crashing it into Paris. The other instance was the Bojinka Plot in 1995 when Ramzi Yousef in the Philippines planned the hijacking of 11 or 12 US aircraft (accounts vary) with the intent of crashing some of them into US targets, including the CIA headquarters at Langley, Virginia.

Turning to who was attacked, the CTC noted that in 2002, there were 199 attacks involving 218 facilities; 111 of these were directed against businesses, 17 against government targets, 14 against diplomats, one against the military, and 75 against 'others' (mainly civilians).

It should be remembered that the CTC only aggregates international incidents, that is, where there is more than one country or nationality involved—which as mentioned earlier account for only about 10% of the annual total of terrorist incidents worldwide. The reality is that the world is less interested in, or feels less threatened by, Pakistanis killing Pakistanis or the Chinese killing Uigurs or Tibetans.

In 2002, there were 725 deaths out of a total of 2738 casualties. The casualties comprised 2257 'others' (civilians), 337 government, 83 military, 39 diplomatic and 22 business. The trend has been towards fewer attacks but more casualties.

What examination of the data does show is that civilians and business people are the more likely terrorism victims. (In 2001, the figure of 4348 'other' deaths was a bit misleading because most were actually business people at the World Trade Center.) The main cause of death is bombings, which account for more than 90% of the deaths.

The good news for government personnel is that they are less likely to be killed—but the bad news is that they are more likely to be individually targeted. Those targeted will usually either be senior bureaucrats or government officials working in rural areas.

Intention of terrorist groups

The intent of terrorist group attacks is to:

- undermine the will of the opponent and cause it to surrender or withdraw
- destroy the legitimacy of a government and its ability to function

- underline the vulnerability of the government (or whoever else the adversary might be)
- popularise the terrorists' cause
- gain recruits and attract financial support, and
- provoke government responses that will alienate and polarise the population.

I will look at the use of bombs in depth in the next chapter but will look here at the other common attack methods used by terrorists.

Hijacking

Hijacking can be of any form of transport, and has included, in the past, trains, ships and smaller vessels, aircraft and buses. It is mainly undertaken to attract media attention, to gain safe passage away from an incident or as an inadvertent consequence of an attack going wrong. Hijacking is now high risk for the perpetrators. Western counterterrorism forces are highly skilled and well equipped to deal with hijackings, and have a good success rate. Trains are particularly hard for terrorists to defend, and we have seen no train hijackings since two in the Netherlands, in 1975 and 1977. The first of the Dutch hijacks saw the government give in to the Moluccan terrorists. The second time the government adopted a hardline policy and used the Dutch marines to resolve the situation and kill the terrorists.

Hostage taking

Kidnapping or hostage-taking may be intended to embarrass or pressure governments. This kind of activity can be hard to deal with when the location of the hostages is not known so rescue is made difficult.

During the late 1980s and early 1990s, the Lebanese Hezbollah held a number of Western hostages in Beirut, including 18 Americans, one of whom, Terry Anderson, was held for six years. The United States was impotent to act because it lacked the intelligence information it needed to locate the hostages. The hostages were eventually released in return for concessions, including to Hezbollah's state sponsor, Iran.

The overall effect of the hostage-taking was to make successive US administrations look impotent. It can also be used to provide bargaining leverage, gain publicity, or raise money.

Areas where kidnapping is currently most prevalent are Africa, Eastern Europe, the Middle East, Pakistan, the Philippines, South America, and Yemen.

Suicide terrorists are a major concern because they may be prepared to die with their hostages to get what they want. The Chechens who took the Moscow theatre patrons hostage in October 2002 created the impression that they were prepared to die if they did not get what they wanted, by wiring up the theatre with explosives. The Russian security forces' bloody resolution of the siege left the question of whether a negotiated settlement might have been possible, unanswered. The tragedy was that the incompetent and heavy-handed Russian response resulted in the deaths of 124 of the 800 plus hostages

Arson

Arson is generally used to destroy infrastructure, and shops and homes of rival ethnic or religious groups. It is sometimes hard to distinguish from insurance fraud, since failing ethnic businesses will sometimes blame rival ethnic groups for destroying their premises. It is easy for fire investigators to recognise an arson attack, but much harder to prove who did it. In the recent past, the Kurdistan Workers Party (PKK) commonly used arson (mainly against Turkish businesses) in Germany until the Germans warned the PKK that if it persisted, Germany would deport Kurdish immigrant workers. Other groups using arson include the Provisional Irish Republican Army (against British and Protestant-owned businesses), Spain's ETA, right-wing and single-issue motivated groups, and rioting mobs in India and Pakistan.

Firebombing

Firebombing is distinguished from arson because it uses an explosive device. Terrorists have commonly firebombed in Northern Ireland, Spain, Germany, Turkey, and the Philippines. In Northern Ireland, a regular PIRA tactic was to tape a can of petrol to the window bars of a target building, often a Protestant pub, then place an explosive charge on the outside of that. The explosion would blast blazing petrol throughout the premises. Terrorist firebombing is often difficult to distinguish from criminal attacks—intended to destroy rival criminal enterprises, 'send a message', or to punish for non-payment of protection money.

Armed attacks

Armed attacks are usually carried out against infrastructure, transport, groups of people, or individuals. Targeted infrastructure might include government buildings, power generation facilities, police stations, law courts and airports. Transport may be attacked to destroy a government's ability to provide public services or support military operations.

Targeted groups of people usually have a defining characteristic—such as, they are: rival ethnic or religious groups; government troops or employees, particularly police; foreign tourists or company employees.

Individuals who are targeted may be symbolically representative of a group—such as national leaders, judges, prominent businesspeople, senior government officials, and politicians—or may be targeted because they are suspected informants or have defected from the terrorist group. (Governments may of course themselves target known terrorists and supporters, or outspoken opponents, for assassination.)

Other attacks

Other forms of attack may include cyber attack, sabotage (sugar in petrol etc), poisoning, use of chemical or biological agents, deliberate contamination and the release of research animals.

Terrorist modus operandi is constantly changing and evolving to take account of the response of the terrorists' adversaries and counter-terrorism capabilities—hence there are now fewer siege hostage situations or politically motivated aircraft hijacks. Terrorists will copy other groups' operations where these have been successful. Because of a decline in state sponsorship, non-Muslim terrorists will increasingly engage in crime to fund their terrorist activities. (Note, however that Muslim terrorists have other sources of income, which are discussed in Chapter Nine.)

CHAPTER SIX
BOMBS AND EXPLOSIVES

Bombings and firebombings are the most common form of terrorist incident, accounting annually, as noted earlier, for 65–75% of all international terrorist attacks. The data is not available to indicate whether this holds true for non-international terrorism but, in any case, international terrorism is a more pressing concern for Western nations.

The first known terrorist use of explosives was the attempt in 1605 by Guy Fawkes, one of a group of Papist plotters, to blow up the British Houses of Parliament.

Bomb making and detonation

Since the early 1990s, the Internet has placed bomb-making information at the disposal of anyone who might want to make a bomb. The Internet also gives useful information on initiators, timing devices, and even on the standard operating procedures (SOPs) of emergency services. It also gives terrorist groups the opportunity to compare notes through email.

There are three main types of explosives:

- low—the black powder used in fireworks
- high—military explosives and
- blasting agents—including 'agricultural' mixes, such as Ammonium Nitrate Fuel Oil (ANFO) mix.

Terrorists will use whatever is most conveniently to hand but preference will always be given to military explosives because they are more powerful and less bulky. Terrorist use of military explosives will suggest access to military supplies or state sponsorship.

Terrorists operating in different areas and conditions will have access to different types of explosives. For example, mining areas will contain blasting agents, detonators and other explosives-related equipment. Urban areas provide access to industrial chemicals, such as chlorates that can be used to make explosive mixes. The effects of a blast may be enhanced by the addition of gas cylinders, sugar, aluminium powder and flammable liquids.

Explosives need an initiator and there are various initiating options available including:

- instantaneous—command detonated
- delay timer—usually based on a mechanical or electronic clock, chemical delay, barometric or altitude switch
- tilt switch—that functions when the bomb is tilted (a favourite for targeting car passengers)
- booby trap—as in a parcel bomb
- photoelectric cell—that operates when a beam is broken (its normal use is in shops to alert staff of incoming customers)
- pressure—that initiates when compressed by a person or vehicle
- magnetic field—set off by a large metal object, like a car, and
- mobile (cellular) phone or pager.

Virtually any remote activating device (such as a garage door opener) can be adapted to initiate an explosion, but it will preferably have a good stand-off distance. For example, the remote control for a model aircraft would be an effective initiator.

Bombs that are factory manufactured for military use are referred to as explosive ordnance, while devices that are manufactured by terrorists or individuals are referred to as improvised explosive devices (IEDs). These homemade devices can be produced to suit the environment or conceal their intent. An IED could therefore be in various forms such as a musical birthday card, parcel, shopping bag, briefcase, suitcase, household item like a radio or toy, pipe bomb (pipe bombs are said to be an invention that dates from the Australian 19th century Eureka stockade revolt), vehicle bomb (bicycle, motorcycle, car, truck, boat), landmine or directional mine, such as the Claymore.

Directional mines like the Claymore are intended to throw blast and shrapnel in a particular direction. Their normal military use is to create a killing zone in ambushes or to protect one's flanks. Claymores were first used in the Korean War against massed Chinese attacks. The Oklahoma bomber, Timothy McVeigh, is believed to have used large drums, containing ammonium nitrate fuel oil mix, laid out in a V pattern within the bomb vehicle to enhance the blast effect.

Other categories of IED are incendiary devices and homemade variants of military items, such as mortar bombs and rockets. Incendiaries are mainly used to destroy commercial premises and seldom cause loss of life.

Some different types of bombs

Many different types of bombs are used by terrorists, depending on the materials available to them and what they hope to achieve from an attack.

One category of bomb that can be particularly deadly is the **human bomb** where terrorists or politically motivated individuals are themselves the bomb carrier. Human bombs have a good chance of success because even if they do not make it all the way to the preferred target, they are still likely to kill security screeners on the way to the target.

Human suicide bombs are used by a number of groups, mainly Muslim: Lebanese Hezbollah (always uses males); Hamas in Israel (usually males); Palestinian Islamic Jihad in Israel (always males); Al Aqsa Martyrs Brigade (Fatah) in Israel (usually males); Ansar al-Islam in Iraq (always males); PKK in Turkey (usually females); Tamil Tigers in Sri Lanka and India (males and females); and Chechen insurgents in Chechnya and Russia (males and females).

Human bombs have been used against specific human targets, as with the assassination of Indian Prime Minister Rajiv Gandhi in 1991. An additional category is those who drive or convey a vehicle bomb to its point of detonation and martyr themselves to ensure success. The most successful example is the September 11 hijackers.

Another category of bomb is the **letter bomb**. Letter bombs cause limited damage and are mainly intended to injure or kill the recipient. Parcel bombs, depending on size, cause more damage and are usually directed at a group or organisation, such as a police station, business, political party or infrastructure.

Portable bombs secreted, for example, in shopping bags, briefcases, or suitcases, may be directed against public gatherings such as markets, or public transport. They are intended to reduce the public will to resist the terrorists, undermine national morale, and underline the impotence of the authorities. The authorities' response, which may involve searching all shopping bags (as is done at Israeli shopping malls) will, in most countries, tend to irritate the public and soon be seen as an unnecessary inconvenience.

Large **vehicle bombs** are used mainly against symbolic infrastructure—such as the attacks against the World Trade Center in New York, the London financial district, the US federal government building in Oklahoma City, or diplomatic missions. If ammonium nitrate fuel oil mix is used against such targets, the amount of ammonium nitrate needed to cause large-scale property damage will make the use of a large, van-like vehicle unavoidable.

Success with a vehicle bomb is more likely if the attacker is prepared for self-sacrifice, one example being the vehicle bomb attack on the US Marine Corps barracks in Lebanon in October 1983 that killed 241 marines. Terrorists will sometimes need to use innocuous vehicles, known as 'blockers', that are parked during quiet periods to save a spot for the bomb vehicle.

Bomb attacks against passenger aircraft can be particularly devastating, leading to total loss of the aircraft and large numbers of casualties. Often a bomb will be timed to detonate over the sea to obscure the evidence.

In the case of the Lockerbie bombing the device was timed to detonate over the Atlantic Ocean, but because of the flight's delayed departure from Heathrow airport, it detonated over Scotland instead.

Civil passenger aircraft operating internationally may be targeted because they are closely linked with a particular state, for example, British Airways with the United Kingdom, or Qantas with Australia. An attack on a country's aircraft can be a symbolic and more achievable alternative to an attack on that country.

Group versus individual bomb attacks

While most bombings are done by groups, there have been some notable individual bomb makers over the years. The anti-technology Unabomber, Ted Kaczynski, made 16 devices that were handcrafted from varnished wood, homemade explosives, and handmade components. He sent bombs through the mail for 18 years before being arrested in 1996. In May 1998 in California, he was given four consecutive life sentences plus 30 years after a plea bargain which resolved charges related to three deaths and the maiming of two scientists.

In December 1998, Australian Taxation Office staff nationwide were put on alert after 24 letter bombs were found addressed to senior current and former employees, and Human Rights and Equal Opportunity Commission staff. One device had earlier exploded in the Canberra mail sorting office. A total of 28 devices were posted. This seems to be a world record for simultaneous bomb mailings. Colin George Dunstan was arrested and sentenced to nine years jail on 26 April 2000, with a minimum non-parole period of five years. His motive was anger with authorities over the way his grievances had been handled.

In March 1999, an Austrian court jailed for life serial letter bomber, Franz Fuchs. He was responsible for 23 letter bombs between 1993 and 1995, which killed at least four people. He claimed to be acting for the fictitious Bavarian Liberation Army. He blew a hand off the Vienna mayor in December 1993 and blew off his own hands in October

1997—which led to his capture. He was sent to a jail for the mentally unbalanced and killed himself in jail on 27 February 2000.

In December 2001, British citizen Richard C Reid, also known as Abdel Rahim, was convicted of trying to blow up an American Airlines aircraft en route from Paris to Miami. The plane's flight crew and passengers subdued him after he tried to ignite explosives built into his shoes. Matches that had been hidden in his shoes had become damp and would not ignite. Reid is suspected of being an Al Qaeda operative known as Abdul Ra'uff. In January 2003, a US court sentenced him to life in prison.

Advantages and disadvantages of bombs for terrorists

Some of the **advantages** of bombs are that they can be:

- spectacular and hence newsworthy
- set to cause a desired level of infrastructure damage
- set to target an individual or a group
- set to allow the attackers to escape or remain undetected
- time-flexible
- remotely detonated
- made with readily available chemicals
- disruptive, with minimal casualties—or used to cause large loss of life
- relatively cheap
- used to make the authorities seem ineffectual
- used to disperse radioactive or non-fissile material
- disowned if there is a botch-up or unintended outcome, and
- readily hoaxed.

Terrorists can disrupt normal activities by simply making a credible threat of a bomb being in place, without actually needing to do anything—but the terrorists need to have a track record of previous bombings, or some evidence of having a workable device. The Provisional IRA disrupted the British national horseracing institution, the Grand National, in 1997 by claiming that they had planted a bomb, or bombs, at the racecourse. No devices were found.

Bombs do have some **disadvantages**, in that:

- they have to be conveyed to the scene
- they can be dangerous to handle—with many cases of accidental initiation or 'own goals'
- they are indiscriminate in terms of victims
- they leave the bomb maker's 'signature'
- they risk alienating the cause's supporters, particularly if the victims are women, children, or animals
- the bomb maker needs a secure location to build the bombs
- they require a skilled craftsperson to make them if they are sophisticated, and
- they leave an audit trail of the components used.

The results of a bomb attack

The casualties of a bomb attack are mainly caused by the blast itself and by flying debris (particularly shards of glass) or by material contained within the bomb and intended to cause casualties (such as nails or ball-bearings). After the Oklahoma bombing in 1995, shards of glass were found embedded in concrete walls up to a block away.

There may also be property damage, including structural damage, and fire is a potential outcome. The Bali bomb was apparently mixed so as to cause heat and fire as well as blast effects.

There will obviously be disruption to normal activities in the area in which the bomb is detonated. In Israel, the bomb squads have only eight hours to examine the scene before it is returned to normal use. Emergency services will of course converge on the bomb scene;

sometimes a small bomb may be used to draw in police, military, and emergency services as the target for a second, much larger, device.

Increased air pressure from a bomb significantly affects the human body. Normal air pressure is 14.7 pounds per square inch (or 101.2 kpa). If that increases by 5–8 pounds the eardrums perforate, and an increase by 10–15 pounds causes the lungs to collapse, which can cause death. The effect of a blast depends on the proximity, size and position of the explosion to a person. Limbs will be torn off and, in a severe case, the only readily identifiable part of the body may be the head, as is often the case with suicide bombers.

Secondary fragments are likely to cause the most carnage. A short increase in distance from the blast scene can dramatically reduce the danger from blast overpressure.

Body fragments from an infected suicide bomber or victims can create an additional hazard from the spread of AIDS or Hepatitis B. Also, rat poison (an anti-coagulant) is sometimes mixed with the explosive to cause victims to bleed to death.

Those investigating an attack will face a number of difficulties, including that the forensic evidence of a bomb attack may be scattered over a large area, and toxic gases or other toxic chemicals may be present in confined spaces. Investigators give a very high priority to the collection of explosive residue and minute bomb particles in proximity to the explosion. The blast crater and human bodies (both dead and wounded) are likely to contain evidentiary material.

Some other considerations for bomb scene examiners are that the bomb scene may be dangerous due to structural instability or ruptured gas mains. Inhalation of atomised body contents, particularly in confined areas, may cause long-term health effects, and emergency personnel may suffer long-term trauma due to the horrendous injuries of the victims.

There may be jurisdictional issues for those investigating a bomb attack, particularly if an aircraft is involved and, in overseas bombings, there can also be sovereignty issues to take into account. The Bali bombing investigation was a good example of cooperative effort, with the Indonesian police using their local knowledge to best effect, and the Australian Federal Police providing sophisticated technological support.

Police need to be aware of the potential for cross-contamination if the same emergency services visit multiple bomb scenes. This could later jeopardise a prosecution. Bomb scene evidence collection is a highly specialised activity and evidence may be useless if the sampling was poor, control samples were not taken, contamination could have occurred, analytical processes were poorly conducted, and findings were open to question.

In conclusion, bombs are a cheap and flexible attack option, with relatively few major disadvantages for the terrorist. Bombs will therefore remain the most popular terrorist attack option—and terrorists will continually seek to produce more capable devices. The latest test bed for new and more capable devices is Iraq where the insurgents are experimenting with new types of remote initiators, roadside bombs, and vehicle bombs in their campaign against coalition forces, non-government organisations and 'traitor' Iraqis.

CHAPTER SEVEN

RELIGIOUS EXTREMISM

This chapter focuses on Muslim extremism, but it should be noted that there are many other forms of religious extremism: Christian (as practised in Northern Ireland and by Right to Life groups in the United States); Jewish (as in Israel); Sikh and Hindu (as seen mainly in India and Sri Lanka); and Buddhist (which tends not to be directed towards others, but rather involves sacrifice of the self.) A desire for a separate state is usually the main driver for religion-linked violence, but religion is a facilitating factor.

Non-Muslim religious extremism

To look at non-Muslim extremism first; Christian terrorism is practised by a number of groups.

In Ireland, both Protestant loyalist groups and Catholic nationalist groups are involved in terrorist activities. One of the factors that the Irish and British governments have in common is that neither of them particularly wants Northern Ireland and its factional baggage.

The Catholic groups are generally dedicated to the reunification of Ireland and to forcing British troops out of Northern Ireland. The Provisional IRA (PIRA), also known as the Provos was formed in 1969 as the clandestine armed wing of Sinn Fein. PIRA has a Marxist orientation and is organised into small, tightly knit cells under the leadership of the Army Council.

The Continuity IRA (CIRA) also known as the Continuity Army Council is a radical terrorist splinter group formed in 1994 as the clandestine armed wing of Republican Sinn Fein (RSF). RSF was formed after the IRA announced a cease-fire in September 1994.

The Real IRA (RIRA) also known as the True IRA was formed in 1998 as the clandestine armed wing of the 32-County Sovereignty Movement, which describes itself as a 'political pressure group'.

On the Protestant side, the Loyalist Volunteer Force (LVF) is a terrorist group formed in 1996 as a faction of the mainstream Protestant Loyalist Ulster Volunteer Force (UVF) but did not emerge publicly until February 1997. It is composed largely of UVF hardliners who have sought to prevent a political settlement with Irish nationalists in Northern Ireland.

The Orange Volunteers (OV) is comprised largely of disgruntled Protestant loyalist hardliners who split from groups observing the cease-fire. OV seeks to prevent a political settlement with Irish nationalists by attacking Catholic civilian interests in Northern Ireland.

Finally in Northern Ireland, the Red Hand Defenders (RHD) is an extremist terrorist group composed largely of Protestant hardliners from those loyalist groups observing a cease-fire. RHD seeks to prevent a political settlement with Irish nationalists by attacking Catholic civilian interests in Northern Ireland.

Jewish terrorism, other than by the state, is manifested by Kach, and Kahane Chai. Their stated goal is to restore the biblical state of Israel. Kach (founded by radical Israeli-American rabbi Meir Kahane) and its offshoot Kahane Chai, which means 'Kahane Lives' (founded by Meir Kahane's son Binyamin, following his father's assassination in the United States), were declared to be terrorist organisations in March 1994 by the Israeli cabinet. This followed the groups' statements in support of Dr Baruch Goldstein's attack in February 1994 on the al-Ibrahimi mosque (Goldstein was affiliated with Kach) and their oral attacks on the Israeli Government. Palestinian gunmen killed Binyamin Kahane and his wife in a drive-by shooting in the West Bank in December 2000.

The most active Hindu terrorist group is the Liberation Tigers of Tamil Eelam (LTTE), better known as the Tamil Tigers. Founded in 1976, the LTTE uses covert and illegal methods to raise funds, acquire weapons, and publicise its aim of establishing an independent Tamil state in Sri Lanka. The LTTE began its armed conflict with the Sri Lankan Government in 1983 and relies on a guerrilla strategy that includes the use of terrorist tactics. It is currently in a Norway-brokered cease-fire with the government.

Cults

Religious cults can turn to violence and the main category of concern is doomsday/destructive/apocalyptic cults (only a very small percentage of religious cults worldwide fall into this category). Others that can cause security problems include the White Supremacist groups, such as the Ku Klux Klan, World Church of the Creator, Aryan Nation, and potentially violent religious cults, such as Concerned Christians and the House of Yahweh.

Destructive cults may direct their violence against the public or against their own members. Groups that have directed violence against the public include Charles Manson's group, The Family, in California in the 1960s, and the 1990s Japanese Aum Shinrikyo (now Aleph) cult. Those that have perpetrated suicides or homicides of their own members include the Branch Davidians, Heaven's Gate, the Movement for the Restoration of the Lord's Commandments, The People's Temple (Jim Jones), and the Solar Temple. The Movement for the Restoration of the Ten Commandments of God in Uganda, was responsible for the death of more than 1000 of its followers in 2000. The second largest cult-related death toll was the previously mentioned, People's Temple group-suicide at Jonestown, Guyana in November 1978, that resulted in the death of 913 followers.[14]

Despite the ongoing threat from non-Muslim groups, Muslim extremism stands out today because of its geographic spread, international dimensions, lethal nature of its attacks, and number of innocent victims.

A brief history and summary of Islam

Islam is one of the world's three major monotheistic religions; the others being Christianity and Judaism. All three have suffered violent internal disputes. They have also clashed with each other, and with other religions.

Islam was founded in Arabia by the prophet Mohammed (570–632) in the 7th century based on revelations he received when the archangel Gabriel appeared to him in a vision. Mohammed was aged 40 at the time. Islam means in the Koran, surrender to the will of Allah (God). The Koran is regarded as the word of God. Another fundamental source of doctrine is the Sunna, claimed to be based on what Mohammed said or did.

Islam emphasises strict religious practices. In the main it is a demanding, but not aggressive, religion, preaching tolerance and peaceful coexistence. Muslims worldwide have a sense of common faith and community. In the Muslim world, the rights of the individual have always been regarded as less important than maintaining traditional values. Rulers have often been autocratic, holding the power of life and death over their subjects.

The five tenets of Islam are:

- the Tawheed, or the oneness of God—'There is no God but God and Mohammed is his prophet'
- to observe the five daily prayers
- to pay the zakat tax for the poor
- to fast from daybreak to sunset during Ramadan, and
- to perform the hajj to Mecca once in one's lifetime—if you can afford it and are physically able to.

One of the most important concepts of Islam is the Sharia, or the Islamic law, under which punishment can be levied by religious courts for adultery, among other things. A fatwa, which is a religious ruling or order, can also be used to direct or encourage violence. Under the fatwa Iranian leader Ayatollah Khomeini levelled at Salman Rushdie after publication of Rushdie's novel, *The Satanic Verses*, in 1988, Muslims were encouraged to kill Rushdie, and there have been several unsuccessful attempts.

Historically, despite the notion of Islamic community, violent internal differences have always existed.

In the 7th century a group of Muslims known as the Kharajis interpreted the Koran as permitting jihad (holy militancy) against the caliph (or head of the Muslim state)—they were wiped out by the 9th century.

The Shiite branch of Islam developed in the 7th century as an outcome of a dispute over the political succession to the prophet Mohammed. It slowly adopted a doctrine of esoteric knowledge based on the imam or exemplary leader—through whom the Koran's truths were said to have been revealed.

The Mu'tazilah (Seceders) in the 9th century saw Allah as incidental to religious fulfilment. Reaction against Mu'tazilism in the 10th century led to Sunni or orthodox theology—which condemned schisms and promoted a sense of Islamic community.

The Nizari Ismailites (11th to 13th centuries) or Assassins were a devout and small sect which wanted to set up a new and vigorous Islamic state under their own imam. As mentioned in Chapter One, they fought their enemies subtly through assassination.

Conflict between Christianity and Islam occurred during the 11th to 14th centuries; Christian crusades were mounted against the Seljuk Turks in what is now Palestine over their prevention of Christian pilgrims from visiting the Holy Land, and particularly Jerusalem. The Seljuk Turks, coincidentally, also acted as a buffer to prevent the westward spread of more radical Islam.

Today there are more than one billion Muslims and they make up the majority of the population in some 45 countries. Indonesia is the world's most populous Islamic nation and almost as many Muslims live in Indonesia (180 million plus) as in the whole of the Arab world). Islam is the second largest religion in Europe after Christianity. Nearly six million Muslims live in North America. In India and Pakistan there are close to 250 million Muslims. There are nearly as many Muslims in India as there are in Pakistan.

Sunnis or Sunnites today form the largest group of Muslims. While they are generally moderate and pragmatic, some Sunnis are extremists. Sunnis number some 800 million while the 100 million Shiites form the second largest group of Muslims today. (Al Qaeda is almost entirely Sunni.) Shiites form the majority faith in Iran, Iraq, and perhaps Yemen, with adherents in Syria, Lebanon, East Africa, India and Pakistan.

Islam, theoretically at least, guarantees the right of non-Muslims to practise their faith—but they are not openly able to do so in some of the more radical Islamic states. Islamic states can be divided into those that are: Islamic fundamentalist states (like Iran); Islamic monarchies (like Kuwait); tolerant or secular Islamic states (like Malaysia, Indonesia and Iraq (even during Saddam's time)); or those containing strong militant Islamic movements fighting against the established government (Algeria).

Modern Muslim extremism

Modern Muslim extremism is traced by some analysts to the activist Muslim Brotherhood that was founded by Hassan el-Banna in 1928 in the Suez Canal town of Ismailia. Egypt banned the Muslim Brotherhood in 1948 and el-Banna was killed by an Egyptian Government agent in 1949. The Muslim Brotherhood has been persecuted by concerned Egyptian and Arab governments ever since, but still has branches in 70 countries. The Muslim Brotherhood has recently been suspected of carrying out terrorist activities in Afghanistan and Chechnya.

A more modern concern, at least since the 1970s, has been the spread of Wahhabism. Wahhabism is a particularly austere and conservative brand of Islam. The sect is named for Muhammad bin Abd al-Wahhab, an 18th century religious leader, whose descendants helped the House of Saud to unify the Saudi Kingdom in 1932. Saudi Arabia regards Wahhabism as the purest form of Islam and it is the official ideology of the country. Saudi Arabia exports Wahhabism peacefully internationally through religious schools (*madrassas*) and by building mosques. At the same time, Al Qaeda promotes Wahhabism through violence.

While the Wahhabi sect is not traditionally violent, extremists fighting in its name have always been regarded as extremely ferocious and prepared to fight to the death. Wahhabism, in its non-violent and violent forms, is a common thread that links Saudi Arabia to Pakistan, the *madrassas*, Afghanistan, the Taliban,[15] and Al Qaeda.

Radical Islamic fundamentalist states (like Iran) export militant fundamentalism both to their neighbours and further afield. As noted earlier, more moderate Islamic countries like Saudi Arabia try to spread Islamic teachings through a focus on building mosques abroad or funding and running *madrassas*, but the process is sometimes subverted by extremist teachers. While Saudi Arabia is a moderate state, it turned a blind eye to the activities of extremists, including Al Qaeda, within its borders, until they started to threaten the stability of the state.

Muslim extremists are regarded as those with fervent religious beliefs that want to change the present system to a more fundamentalist one through violence.[16] Extremists embrace a concept of jihad under which anyone who dies fighting in a holy war goes straight to heaven. Many are fighting against an adversary to win a homeland, like Lebanese Hezbollah was in Lebanon until the Israeli withdrawal in May 2000, and Hamas is today against Israeli occupation of Palestinian land.

Those martyred through death as part of a jihad are revered, and a number of Muslim sources provide money to the immediate family and free education for a martyr's children, while the close relatives are also guaranteed access to heaven. In addition, in heaven the male martyr is said to be lavishly feted and has all he can eat and drink. It is less clear what benefits accrue to female martyrs. They are usually motivated by nationalism or revenge, rather than potential personal benefits.

The United States and the West have tended to support traditional Muslim rulers, who are usually conservative and not much interested in social progress for the general population. The West prefers them because they provide a reasonably stable basis for economic or strategic association, and arms sales. This has fostered street level rebellion and even frustrated the educated middle classes who are blocked from higher office and effecting political changes.

The Iranian revolution in 1978–79 provided a model for fundamentalists in other states of a modern Islamic fundamentalist state, with its authoritarian emphasis on identity, culture, political participation, and social justice—and rejection of Westernisation and government authoritarianism, corruption, and unequal distribution of wealth.

In Afghanistan, the Taliban were to establish an even more fundamentalist state than Iran's was in 1979. In August 1994, a senior mullah in Kandahar, Mohammad Omar Akhund, established the Taliban, a group of Sunni Deobandi religious students, who quickly became an effective guerilla force. By September 1996, they had taken Kabul and declared Afghanistan a fundamentalist Islamic state.

The terrorist threat from Islamic states

The United States has for many years considered five Muslim countries to be a terrorism security threat as state sponsors of terrorism. These are Iran, Iraq, Libya, Sudan, and Syria. Since the United States has occupied and run Iraq, it will presumably soon be taken off the list.

In 2003, Libya publicly owned up to its possession of weapons of mass destruction and is hoping, mainly for trade reasons, to be accepted back into the international community. Colonel Gaddafi is also concerned about the potential threat to his rule from Al Qaeda.

Iran has in the past been involved in the planning and execution of terrorist acts by its own agents and by surrogates such as Hezbollah groups. It continues to fund and train Shiite terrorist groups, particularly the Lebanese Hezbollah.

Although Iraq had acted in the past against Iraqi dissidents abroad, its main focus has been on support for Palestinian groups, many of whom have maintained offices in Baghdad. The alleged Iraqi plot to assassinate former President Bush in 1993 in Kuwait does not seem to have much credence. Kuwait's creative reporting of the details to the United States was probably to gain favour with the Clinton administration. Iraq also allowed the anti-Iranian Mujahedin-e Khalq Organisation (MEK or MKO) to base itself in Iraq and conduct operations against Iran from Iraq.

There is no evidence of Iraqi cooperative links with Al Qaeda or of Iraqi involvement in the September 11 attacks, but it seems likely that there has been informal contact over the years between the Iraqi intelligence service and Al Qaeda. These contacts have been well documented by the United States since the war in Iraq but they probably amounted mainly to Saddam keeping a watchful eye on a group that could potentially cause him problems.

Libya, despite the Pan Am flight 103 and French UTA flight 772 trial outcomes (UTA 772, en route from Brazzaville in the Congo to Charles de Gaulle airport in Paris, was blown up over the Sahara desert in 1989, killing all 170 passengers and crew), had maintained that it was not involved in the Lockerbie bombing. In 2003, it acknowledged responsibility and agreed to pay compensation to the victims' families, but this could be to regain access to the world oil market. In 2000, it tried to improve its image internationally by paying ransom money to the Philippines Abu Sayyaf Group to secure the release of Western hostages.

Libya still provides support to a variety of Palestinian terrorist groups, including the Abu Nidal Organisation (ANO), the Palestine Islamic Jihad (PIJ), and Ahmad Jibril's Popular Front for the Liberation of Palestine—General Command (PFLP-GC).

Sudan continues to be used as a safe haven by members of various groups, including Al Qaeda, the Egyptian al-Gama'a al-Islamiyya (IG), Egyptian Islamic Jihad (EIJ), PIJ, and Hamas. Most of these groups use Sudan primarily as a base for assisting compatriots elsewhere.

Syria continues to provide safe haven and support to several terrorist groups, some of which maintain training camps or other facilities on Syrian territory. The PFLP-GC, PIJ, Abu Musa's Fatah-the-Intifada, and George Habash's PFLP maintain their headquarters in Damascus. Syria grants Hamas, the PFLP-GC, and the PIJ basing privileges and refuge in the areas of Lebanon's Bekaa Valley that are under Syrian control.

Iran, Iraq, and Libya were at one time engaged in the assassination of outspoken expatriates living abroad, but there have been no known assassinations since 1993.

Notable omissions from the US sponsors of terrorism list are Lebanon, Pakistan, and Saudi Arabia, all of whom have provided active or passive support to terrorists:

- Lebanon does little to stop terrorists from operating within the areas it controls
- Pakistan sponsors terrorism into India (its Inter-Services Intelligence (ISI) provides support to Mujaheddin operating into Kashmir and provides them with military explosives), and
- Saudi Arabia provides funds to promote Wahhabism, some of which ends up funding terrorism. Agents of the Saudi government and some rich Saudis have also provided funding and support for Al Qaeda.

Middle East extremist terrorist groups

Some prominent Middle East Muslim terrorist groups are Lebanese Hezbollah (Party of God); Hamas, which is the Arabic acronym for 'The Islamic Resistance Movement' (Harakat al-Muqawamah al-Islamiyya); the PIJ; the Algerian Armed Islamic Group (AIG or GIA); the Egyptian IG and EIJ and; the anti-Iranian Mujahedin-e Khalq Organisation (MEK or MKO).[17]

Many Muslim terrorist groups have spiritual leaders, such as Algeria's Abdel Rahman al-Zaytouni, the Egyptian organisations' Sheikh Omar

Abdel Rahman, Hezbollah's Sheikh Mohammed Hussein Fadlallah or Jemaah Islamiah's Abu Bakar Bashir.

Both Egyptian groups regard Sheikh Omar Abdel Rahman, jailed in the United States for his involvement in planning terrorist attacks in New York, as their spiritual leader. The goal of both Egyptian factions is to overthrow the government of President Hosni Mubarak and replace it with a fundamentalist Islamic one.

The most important terrorism development in recent years has been Osama bin Laden's creation of a pan-Islamic terrorist movement that embraces all Muslims (although, of course the vast majority of Muslims do not condone Al Qaeda's activities).

The anti-Soviet war in Afghanistan during 1979–88 created a generation of respected jihadis; many of whom are now linked to Al Qaeda. The veterans include an estimated 5000 Saudis, 3000 Yemenis, 2800 Algerians, 2000 Egyptians, 2000 Palestinians, 1000 South-East Asians, as well as Jordanians, Lebanese, Iranians, Tunisians, Iraqis, Libyans and others. In addition, 20,000 fighters are believed to have passed through Al Qaeda training camps post-1996.[18] Thousands are active in Bosnia, Chechnya, Dagestan, Soviet Asia—particularly Tajikistan; and Algeria, Yemen, Egypt, and the Arabian Peninsula.

Osama bin Laden established Al Qaeda in 1989 to bring together Muslims who had fought in Afghanistan against the Soviet invasion. His aim was to establish a pan-Islamic caliphate 'from Morocco to Mindanao' by working with Muslim extremist groups to overthrow regimes he deemed 'non-Islamic' and to expel Westerners and non-Muslims from Muslim countries. In February 1998, bin Laden announced the formation of a 'World Islamic Front for Jihad Against the Jews and Crusaders'. Those who participated in the announcement, in addition to bin Laden as the leader of Al Qaeda, were the leaders of the EIJ and IG of Egypt, Pakistan's Jamiat-ul-Ulema-e-Pakistan (JU), and the Jihad Movement in Bangladesh (BJ). At the same time, bin Laden announced a fatwa against the United States and the Israelis for their occupation of holy places in the Middle East—the fatwa included civilians.

The key to Al Qaeda's durability is its network structure, its ability to replace lost leaders, and its non-reliance on territory or a geographical base. It acts as the violent vanguard for a fundamentalist, anti-Western (particularly American and Jewish) movement. Like all great movements, it is driven by the power of a compelling ideology, in this case a desire to return Islam to its roots and remove corrupting Western influences.

Other Muslim extremist groups

There are a number of prominent Muslim extremist groups operating in areas other than the Middle East.

The Harakat ul-Mujahidin (HUM) was formerly known as the Harakat al-Ansar (HUA). The HUM is a Muslim militant group based in Pakistan that operates primarily in Kashmir. The long-time leader of the group, Fazlur Rehman Khalil, stepped down in 2000, with his popular second-in-command, Farooq Kashmiri taking over as leader.

The Lashkar-e-Tayyiba (pronounced Toyba) (LT, Army of the Righteous or Army of the Pure) is the armed wing of the Pakistan-based religious organisation, Markaz-ud-Dawa-wal-Irshad (MDI), a Sunni anti-US missionary organisation formed in 1989. LT is one of the three largest and best-trained groups fighting in Kashmir against India and is not connected to a political party. The LT leader is Abdul Wahid Kashmiri.

Jaish-e-Mohammed (JEM) (Army of Mohammed) is a Muslim extremist group based in Pakistan that has rapidly expanded in size and capability since it was formed by Maulana Masood Azhar, a former HUA leader, in February 2000. The group's aim is to unite Kashmir with Pakistan. It is politically aligned with the radical, pro-Taliban, political party, Jamiat-i Ulema-i Islam Fazlur Rehman faction (JUI-F). JEM has been linked to the kidnapping and murder of *The Wall Street Journal* reporter Daniel Pearl in 2003.

The Islamic Movement of Uzbekistan (IMU) is a coalition of Muslim militants from Uzbekistan and other central Asian states opposed to Uzbekistani President Islam Karimov's secular regime. Their main goal is the establishment of an Islamic state in Uzbekistan. The group's propaganda also includes anti-Western and anti-Israeli rhetoric.

As mentioned in Chapter Two, the Abu Sayyaf Group (ASG) is the smallest and most radical of the Muslim separatist groups operating in the southern Philippines. Some ASG members fought and trained in Afghanistan during 1979–88. The group split from the Moro National Liberation Front in 1991 under the leadership of former Afghanistan Mujaheddin fighter, Abdurajak Abubakar Janjalani. He was killed in a clash with Filipino police in December 1998. Some reports place his younger brother, Khadafi Janjalani, as the nominal leader of the group, which now seems to be composed of several factions. While most of its victims are Filipino Christians, ASG has been involved in the kidnapping and murder of Westerners, particularly Americans, in the Philippines and is believed to have been linked in the past to Al Qaeda, but it largely has placed itself outside the jihad movement in recent years by its criminal activities for personal gain.

The South African group People Against Gangsterism and Drugs (PAGAD) was formed in 1996 as a community anti-crime vigilante group fighting drugs and violence in Cape Town. By early 1998 it had also become anti-government and anti-Western. PAGAD views the South African Government as a threat to Islamic values and promotes a greater political voice for South African Muslims. Abdus Salaam Ebrahim leads the group. PAGAD's G-Force (Gun Force) operates in small cells and is believed responsible for carrying out acts of terrorism. PAGAD uses several front names.

Targets of Muslim terrorist groups

The targets of the Muslim terrorist groups vary. The Egyptian group, IG, has targeted leaders and officials, sometimes when overseas. Of particular note are the attempt on Egyptian President Mubarak in Ethiopia in

June 1995 and the attack on the Egyptian embassy in Islamabad, Pakistan in November 1995.

Most Muslim terrorist groups will target US nationals when the opportunity arises. This is mainly because of the United States' support for Israel and because the United States is seen as an exploitative enemy of Muslim interests. Israelis or Jews are regarded as even more desirable targets. American journalist Daniel Pearl might have survived had not a Pakistani journalist revealed that he was Jewish.

The Pakistani groups mainly target non-Muslims and Indian military forces in Indian-occupied Kashmir. Elsewhere, civilians transmigrated to Muslim separatist areas to increase central government control have been targeted, as in Xinjiang by Uigur separatists, in the Philippines by the Moros, and in Aceh by the Free Aceh Movement (or GAM). Officially sponsored transmigration of heartland population to potential breakaway provinces is a common way for governments to try to undermine separatist sentiments and make the dissident population a minority in its own area. Any 'democratic' plebiscite for independence will then be unsuccessful.

As noted earlier, Muslim separatists may not be primarily motivated by religious beliefs. Their main motivation may be nationalism, separatism, or reaction to discrimination. Being Muslim however provides them with a means of gaining external support, including funding, weapons and training, from external Muslim sympathisers.

Muslim extremists in South-East Asia are said to support the notion of a multi-country pan-Islamic state in South-East Asia. Sekarmaji Marijan Kartosuwiryo, one of the founders of the Islamic State of Indonesia, first articulated this concept in 1949. The state would include Indonesia, Malaysia, Singapore, Brunei, plus parts of southern Thailand, Cambodia and the southern Philippines.

In the future, Muslim extremism will continue to exist in several forms: as a way of promoting extremist and fundamentalist religious beliefs and opposing more moderate forms of Islam; as a common cause against perceived injustice; to support breakaway elements (as with the Kosovars in the Balkans); and as a focus for opposing the

'Great Satan' (the United States) and its friends. As the United States arrests and jails more Muslim extremists, the United States will increasingly become more of a target.

Some of the future Muslim extremist attacks—against the United States in particular—will be by 'loners', sympathetic either to the Palestinian cause, or to Islamic causes in general. Security intelligence will find it difficult to prevent such attacks because of the lack of intelligence indicators that would be provided by group membership.

Osama bin Laden's and the Egyptian Dr Ayman al-Zawahiri's videotapes and audiotapes are increasingly influential in the Muslim-majority countries in identifying the Western countries that are aligned against the Muslim world. Countries like the United Kingdom and Australia, and their citizens overseas, are at a higher level of risk because of this increased attention.

CHAPTER EIGHT

CYBERTERRORISM AND TERRORIST USE OF E-SYSTEMS

Cyberterrorism is politically motivated electronic attacks, intended to shock and terrify, directed mainly against non-combatant areas to achieve a strategic outcome. An example might be the opening of dam gates electronically to cause widespread flooding. There have been no instances of terrorist groups using electronic systems for terrorism to date, but intelligence projections over recent years have consistently assessed a high risk of future terrorist cyberattack.

During 2002, police in California began investigating a suspicious pattern of surveillance against Silicon Valley computers. Unknown persons in the Middle East and South Asia were exploring the digital systems used to manage Bay Area utilities. An FBI investigation found that there had been 'multiple casings of sites' nationwide. Emergency telephone systems, electrical generation and transmission, water storage and distribution, nuclear power plants and gas facilities had all been examined. The probes had been routed through telecommunications switches in Saudi Arabia, Indonesia and Pakistan. Some of the probes suggested planning for a conventional attack, but others homed in on a class of digital devices that allow remote control of services such as fire despatch and equipment like pumps on pipelines. More information about these digital devices, and how to program them, turned up on Al Qaeda computers seized during 2002.

US intelligence analysts believe that by disabling or taking command of the floodgates in a dam, for example, or of substations handling high voltage electric power, an intruder could use virtual tools to destroy lives and property. A concern is that such attacks could be timed to coincide with other, physical attacks to cause maximum effect.

Ronald Dick, director of the FBI's National Infrastructure Protection Centre was quoted as saying 'The event I fear most is a physical attack in conjunction with a successful cyber-attack on the responders' 911 system or on the power grid'.[19]

Manipulation of the remote controls that have been introduced for economic reasons in some industries could cause major problems. In Queensland in April 2000, police stopped a car and found a stolen computer and radio transmitter inside. Using commercially available technology, Vitek Boden had turned his vehicle into a pirate command centre for sewage treatment along Australia's Sunshine Coast. Boden had quit his job at Hunter Watertech, the supplier of Maroochy Shire's remote control and telemetry equipment and apparently decided to sabotage the sewerage system, angling for a consulting contract to solve the problems he had created. Boden set himself up as the central control system during his intrusions, with command of 300 Supervisory Control and Data Acquisition (SCADA) nodes governing sewage and drinking water.

Boden allowed hundreds of thousands of gallons of putrid sludge to flow into parks and rivers. Nearly identical systems run oil and gas utilities and many manufacturing plants. But their most critical use is in the generation, transmission and distribution of electrical power, because electricity has no substitute and every other key element of infrastructure depends upon it.

Massoud Amin, a mathematician directing new security efforts in the US electricity generating industry, described the North American power grid as 'the most complex machine ever built' and agreed that they have no idea how the grid would respond to a cyber-attack.

Joseph Weiss, an expert in control system security, has told industry conferences that intruders were 'able to assemble a detailed map' of each system and 'intercepted and changed' SCADA commands without detection.[20]

Hacking and viruses

There is of course a considerable difference between persons using electronic systems to mount terrorist attacks, and political activists using the Internet to organise demonstrations. The more common type of politically motivated cyberattack has been by hacker activists (hacktivists) supporting anti-globalisation activities or mounting attacks on multinational corporations and government agencies.

In a modern warfare context, computer information attacks are operations to disrupt, sabotage and destroy information in enemy computer network systems using specialised equipment, software, or firepower. Attack forms can include soft kills (electromagnetic jamming, virus insertion) and hard kills (physical destruction). One offensive form is virus sabotage: using computer viruses for information attacks on computers in multiple areas and directions.

Government agencies are always going to be a likely target for electronic attack, as well as multinationals and prominent businesses. Most cyberattacks to date have been by teenage nerds, some of whom have been politically motivated. The United States Government estimated the cost to the United States of identifying and countering electronic attacks in 2001 was US$20 billion. Microsoft's Bill Gates put the cost of hacker attacks in 2001 at US$455 million.[21]

While there have been no cyberterrorism attacks so far, there have been conventional terrorist attacks intended to take down electronic systems. The 1993 London Bishopsgate bombing by the Provisional IRA (PIRA) was directed at London's financial market electronic systems. The September 11 attacks on the World Trade Center had a disruptive effect on business information systems internationally although that was probably not the main intent of the attacks.

Groups that participate in politically motivated violence do however use the Internet and computers for a number of purposes including:

- command and control
- coordination of national and transnational activities
- communication between groups
- public relations
- spreading propaganda about their cause, doctrine or ideology
- publicising information to facilitate violence by others
- acquiring information that will assist terrorist activities (such as information on hacking tools, targets, weapons, CBRN (chemical, biological, radiological and nuclear) devices, and other bomb-making information)
- assessment of vulnerabilities of potential targets (by scanning for program weaknesses)
- recruitment of new members; fundraising; and money laundering.

There are many politically motivated hate sites on the Internet promoting Muslim extremism, Nazism, white supremacy, anti-abortion, Christian extremism, and ethno-nationalism, to cite a few. So-called cybervigilantes or cyberpatriots have taken it upon themselves to advise server operators that they are hosting enemies of society, causing many sites to be closed down. Other sites, such as the English-language web site for the Arabic television network, Al Jazeera, have been repeatedly hacked by cyberpatriots, who do not believe in freedom of speech unless it is pro-United States or pro-Israel. Such activity only removes the sites from public examination and debate, or forces the groups involved to retreat into foreign languages to escape attack.

Types of cyberattack can include: placing bugs in CGI scripts (programs that are written to get a web site to do tasks); deliberately placed trapdoors (a Canadian cryptographer claims that there is a US National Security Agency backdoor to Microsoft Windows that would allow United States Government intelligence agencies to establish covert access; information warfare; extortion (rarely reported); hacking,[22] cracking (hacking with the intent to steal or deface); spamming (swamping with emails);[23] use of rogue programs; and spreading of viruses. There is a lack of data that links such activities to terrorism but the new generation of terrorists is often adept at using computers and it is only a matter of time before we see terrorists engaged in these kinds of activities.

Cyberespionage can also be used by terrorists to gain passwords, gain access to databases and networks, shut down services (and disrupt emergency services to enhance a physical attack), introduce instructions for attacks through logic bombs or Trojan horses,[24] manipulate data, conduct financial fraud, extort money, and, cause Denial of Service (DoS) (due to server overload). Some examples of cyberattack are listed below.

- 'Moonlight Maze' was the name given to successful attacks in 1998 against US Department of Defense systems by Russian Academy of Science hackers. Their motivation is not known.
- In May 1998 US intelligence officials reported the first known attack by a 'terrorist group' on a target country's computer systems. The cyber-strike apparently was little more than a bid by ethnic Tamil guerrillas to swamp Sri Lankan embassies with electronic mail.
- 'Zyklon' (the handle of American teenager Eric Burns) attacked web pages for NATO, the White House, US senate, then US vice-president Al Gore, and the US Information Agency in 1998 and 1999. He also attacked Internet servers. He apparently did it because it was a challenge and to gain stature in the hacker community.
- In the late 1980s and early 1990s, 'Phoenix', an Australian, hacked into the NASA and Lawrence Livermore Laboratories, the Australian Commonwealth Scientific and Industrial Research Organisation (CSIRO), and a major computer business in the United States. He was arrested in Australia and received a suspended sentence. He also did it because it was a challenge.

- 'M1crochip', part of the FOrpaxe group, attacked US government web sites from Portugal in the late 1990s. He was clearly politically motivated but not a terrorist.
- In January 1999, 'E-Nazis' attacked the East Timor Virtual Country domain in Ireland from 18 countries, including Australia. It is believed that the attack originated in Indonesia.
- In February 1999, there were attacks on Japanese Government web sites by Chinese groups protesting the Japanese reinterpretation of the Nanjing massacre. Japanese reinterpretation of its military past for domestic consumption is a continuing sore point with countries that suffered from Japanese occupation during the Second World War.
- In May 1999, after the United States' accidental bombing of the Chinese embassy in Belgrade, hackers (probably Chinese) cracked the US Department of Energy's web site with the message 'Protest USA's Nazi action! Protest NATO's brutal action! ... You have owed Chinese people a bloody debt which you must pay for. We won't stop attacking until the war stops!' This was probably a Chinese Government encouraged protest.
- In August 1999, Russian hackers took down a Dagestan web site established by a Muslim militant group. This was probably done by a government agency.
- Hackers also attacked NATO sites during the 1999 bombing of Serbia. This was organised by the hacker community.
- In September 1999, there was a surge in attacks on Australian government web sites after Australia's East Timor involvement. It is not clear who was responsible but Australia was seen to have encouraged the breakaway of part of the Muslim world, even though East Timor is predominantly Christian.
- In 1999, 'flipz', a US teenager, cracked Singapore government web sites as well as United States Department of Defense sites, and Microsoft's own web site (a first).
- In February 2000, hackers used tribal flooding software to harness slave computers to create a ping storm[25] that slowed down major

web sites including Yahoo!, eBay, E*Trade, Buy.com, CNN.com, Amazon.com, ZDNet.com, Datek and Excite.

- In 2002 and 2003, US hackers took down the Al Qaeda web site. The previously mentioned attacks on the Al Jazeera web site were motivated by US claims that Al Jazeera is a mouthpiece for Al Qaeda and anti-Americanism.

One of the most high profile forms of cyberattack involves the release of viruses. Some examples of viruses used for cyberattacks include:

- Bloody 6/4 and Michelangelo, used by Taiwanese students against China in revenge for the 1989 Tiananmen Square massacre.
- PrettyPark which stole data and attached itself to emails.
- Chernobyl was timed to act on 25 April 1998 and recur on the 26th of the month. It was created by a Taiwanese student and attacked computer hard drives.
- The Melissa virus was created and released by American David Smith in March 1999. Smith used email proliferation to attack Microsoft Word and Excel. The damage was estimated at US$80 million and Smith was jailed for 20 months.
- Prilissa, a combination of Melissa and Worm, Explore.Zip or MiniZip, attached to emails and attacked Microsoft software.
- The 'I Love You' virus spread overnight in May 2000 from the Philippines. The email activated when opened, searched for the user's address book and then sent emails to all the addresses listed. It also had the capability to delete files. Its creator Reomel Ramores was never punished.
- The Kournikova virus of February 2001 had a similar effect in swamping email systems across the world. Its Dutch creator Jan de Wit received 150 hours of community service.

In 2002, it was estimated that viruses infected one in every 212 emails. The technical sophistication of viruses is increasing, and they are increasingly targeting antivirus software and firewalls.

Another problem for computer users is false security warnings. These may warn the user not to open an email with a particular subject line (and to forward the warning to others), or to delete a specific file from their hard drive that can then affect the operating system. It is not clear who originates them or to what purpose.

Some of the many difficulties of dealing with cyberactivism are that such activities are deniable or can be obscured by using multiple transit points.[26] The law is not able to keep up with electronic developments, and police areas are under-resourced and find it hard to attract or retain high calibre electronic investigators.

Decryption of suspect communications is sometimes very difficult, particularly if state-of-the-art encryption software has been used.

Another way of hiding data is steganography—where information is embedded in or behind other data. Paradoxically, standardisation of electronic financial systems has helped facilitate transnational criminal activities. Several Russian criminals have become billionaires through manipulation of the corrupted and subverted Russian financial systems, but to date this kind of manipulation has not been used, as far as is known, to benefit terrorism.

Conventional law enforcement faces difficult jurisdictional issues in dealing with these matters. At one stage the FBI claimed global jurisdiction because the Internet began in the United States. This has however proved fairly meaningless because most other countries have a different view. Governments' legal counterattack options are also limited.

Businesses are particularly vulnerable to electronic attack—only one third of businesses have firewalls and maintain them, or use multiple methods of controlling electronic traffic flows. Firewalls typically use one or more of these methods to control traffic flowing in and out of the network:

- **Packet filtering** Packets of data are analysed. Only packets that make it through the filters are forwarded to the requesting system.
- **Outbound filtering** Some firewalls only work in one direction.

They examine packets a computer is receiving, not the ones it sends. Hostile applications such as trojan horses, worms and viruses can use an Internet connection to send sensitive information from a system. A firewall should at least have a mechanism for filtering outbound traffic.

- **Proxy service** Information from the Internet is retrieved by the firewall and then forwarded to the requesting system and vice versa.
- **Stateful inspection** A method that compares certain key parts of a packet to a database of trusted information. If the comparison yields a reasonable match, the information is allowed through, otherwise it is blocked.

Businesses are resistant for commercial reasons to government regulation or imposed security standards in this area because they often increase costs.

The exponential growth in the Internet and electronic systems will increase national vulnerabilities to cyberattack. The US free speech laws limit the options for restricting 'undesirable' information on the Internet, but the size and transnational nature of the Internet make censorship impractical. Politically motivated web sites can move offshore if pressured.

The United States committed itself to spending US$2 billion on protection of US Government electronic systems in the financial year ending 30 September 2003, which could mean that attackers will focus on softer targets. Australia, among other countries, is aware of its vulnerabilities but the threat is generally perceived (without justification) as lower in Australia than in the United States. Protection of electronic systems is often seen as primarily an agency or business responsibility.

The one piece of good news is that the threat of terrorist attack using electronic systems remains more notional than actual, because terrorists find the Internet useful and do not want to attract governments' attention to their use of it. Should this cease to be the case, there is certainly the potential for terrorists to cause chaos and casualties by, for example, taking down the traffic control systems at a busy airport.

CHAPTER NINE

TERRORISM FINANCING

In the past, much of the financing for global terrorism has not come from illegal activities. Only a very small proportion of global illicit financial transactions (estimated at up to US$1.5 trillion annually) currently finds its way to terrorists.

Factors that are assisting terrorists are, however, similar to the ones facilitating criminal access to financial systems. These include financial globalisation, weak state controls, lax banking regulations, shadowy financial systems, and corruption within financial and political systems. Funds are moved around using unregulated money transfer systems, the Internet, cash, diamonds, gold and other precious metals (mainly through Dubai), the Islamic banking system (particularly through countries like Albania) and the international banking system (particularly through off-shore unregulated centres).

A common unregulated method of transferring terrorist funds is through *hawala* systems. This could, for example, involve money being passed to a *hawaladar* in New York for delivery to a small village in Pakistan. The money does not actually move; there is a periodic 'levelling up' of transfers between *hawaladars* instead. This makes *hawala* transfers very difficult to interdict.

While criminals seek money for enrichment, terrorists seek money to cover operational costs—and terrorists do not need large sums of money as the services of their members are provided free of charge. While weapons and explosives can be expensive, particularly items like surface to air missiles (SAMs), terrorist operations on the whole are very cost-effective. The cost of the 12 October 2000 attack on the USS *Cole* was estimated at US$5000. The *Cole* cost US$280 million to repair.

The cost to Al Qaeda of the 11 September 2001 attacks was estimated to be about US$500,000, including the flying lessons and travel. The United States estimates the cost of the clean-up, property losses and bail-outs at US$135 billion, but the figure would go much higher if all the international impacts were factored in.

The main sources of financing for terrorist groups vary from one group to another, but include funds generated from cooperating with organised crime, including the protection of narcotics traffickers, direct involvement in narcotics trafficking, and funds generated by front companies, business enterprises, charities, donations, sponsors, and wealthy sympathisers.

Several terrorist groups, notably the Revolutionary Armed Forces of Colombia (FARC), the Al Qaeda network and its Chechen allies, various militant groups operating in Pakistan, the Tamil Tigers in Sri Lanka, the Kurdistan Workers Party (PKK) and others, have been engaged in aspects of the lucrative drugs trade. For some groups, involvement with crime has reflected a need for independent funding of terrorist activities following a decline in state sponsorship since about 1990 with the collapse of the Soviet Union.

Other organised crime related activities include smuggling of various kinds, and cooperation with Eastern European mafia groups and other crime organisations where this has been in the interest of both parties. In India, for example, there are reports of terrorists using travel agencies run by organised crime that can provide new identities and any documentation needed for travel.

Meanwhile, right-wing extremists are increasingly funding their activities through the manufacture and sale of amphetamines and designer drugs.

Other types of crime engaged in by terrorists include protection rackets, credit card fraud, kidnap for ransom, extortion, hostage-taking for influence, bank robberies, electronic fraud, trafficking in firearms, sanctions breaking, human smuggling, and sex trafficking.

Al Qaeda's financial structure is said to be based on the four 'C's'—criminal activities, charities, commodities, and companies. Its criminal activities include money laundering, narcotics, arms trafficking, and extortion. Charities used include Blessed Relief, the International Islamic Relief Organisation (IIRO) and Wafa Humanitarian Organisation. Commodities marketed include gum arabic (a key ingredient in soft drinks, like Coca Cola, among other things) and honey. Front companies are believed to include Al Taqwa Management Organisation, Taba Investments, Ariana Afghan Airlines, Wadi al Aqiq, and Bin Laden International.

Groups with large cash flows (like Al Qaeda and the Provisional IRA) have also made long-term business investments that generate licit funds that can be used for terrorist purposes. Osama bin Laden is well versed in this practice from his time as an administrator for the Mujaheddin. He has set up front companies and charities and used other measures to hide the actual ownership of Al Qaeda's funds.

At the other end of the scale are investments by criminal groups (like the Japanese Yakuza and Italian Mafia) that are being used to influence politicians and subvert political processes. However, because these activities are not politically motivated they do not fall within our area of interest.

The funds generated by Muslim zakat (charity) payments are substantial (estimated at US$5–16 billion a year; US$1.6 million in Saudi Arabia each day). Some of the money allocated to good works is diverted to terrorist use (in the cause of jihad violence). This in turn allows movements like Al Qaeda to subsidise regional extremist activity, including in the Philippines and Indonesia.

Expatriate communities are often encouraged to donate to 'the cause' back home. In Western countries, for example, ethnic communities that have come under pressure to donate to violent causes include Arabs, Iranians, the Irish, Kosovo Albanians, Kurds, Lebanese, and Sri Lankan Tamils.

Few states want to be identified as directly funding terrorism, but among those who are believed to fund politically motivated violence are Iran, Israel, Lebanon, Libya, Pakistan, Syria, and Saudi Arabia. If the Bush administration's qualification is applied (a sponsor is any state that is not actively opposing terrorism on its soil or not prepared to prosecute or give up a terrorist wanted by another state)—the list would be much longer, and would include some of the United States' European allies who have not been prepared to allow extradition of terrorism suspects. This is because they are unlikely to be given a fair trial in the United States and could face the death penalty. The United Kingdom, France and Germany are three such countries.

Some groups have wealthy sponsors who provide funds, either because they are coerced to do so, or because they believe in the cause being promoted by the terrorists. An example is the funds provided by wealthy Persian Gulf and Middle Eastern Arabs to support Osama bin Laden's promotion of pan-Islamism and militant Wahhabism.

A new and potentially powerful anti-terrorism measure, the United Nations International Convention for the Suppression of the Financing of Terrorism, came into force on 10 April 2002, after being ratified by more than the required 22 countries. Countries have to bring their national laws into line with the convention's provisions and they are expected to develop and implement mechanisms to meet its standards. For example, they must take measures that would allow 'legal entities' to be held liable for actions taken by a person responsible for the management or control of that entity They must also ensure that criminal acts covered by the convention will not be considered justifiable on political, philosophical, ideological, racial, ethnic or religious grounds.

Some of the concerns that attach to the convention are that, due to the lack of a UN terrorism definition, it could be loosely applied to target ethnic minorities, like the Uigurs, and it could also be used to introduce draconian laws that crack down on anti-government political activity.

The Convention obliges the states that are parties to it to prosecute offenders or extradite them to the signatory countries that suffered from their illegal acts, and assist other states in investigations and preventive efforts.

Another weakness of the UN legislation is that while it commits governments to act, there is no laid down timetable for them to comply. The IMF is trying to push countries to comply and is offering technical assistance to help them. It is also itself assessing the role of offshore financial centres. A powerful lever would be to make IMF loans contingent on compliance (but this is unlikely to happen). Unsurprisingly, sovereign powers usually interpret international laws, treaties and agreements discretely to suit their own national interests.

Even when terrorists are detained, there are sometimes issues related to protection of one's own or other states' nationals from foreign powers. As noted, a country that does not have the death penalty may not give up a person to a country (like the United States), that does.

In reality, the new UN legislation has not hurt Muslim extremists who can still access *hawala* and charity funds that are not easily interdicted by governments. Enforcement of the convention is made more difficult by the fact that terrorists and criminals have in the past moved through jurisdictions with relative ease, while law enforcers are hampered by jurisdictional issues and a lack of uniform laws and legal processes. Similar agencies in different governments often cooperate well—but may find their efforts undermined or unsupported within their own government systems.

CHAPTER TEN

POLITICAL ASSASSINATION

Assassination has a long history and in Chapter One we looked at the Zealot Sicarii campaign against the Romans during 6–73 AD in Palestine, and the activities of the Assassins during 1094–1273. A useful web site for assassination-related topics is provided below.[27]

In the past, ninjas were employable assassins in Japan. In the 1890s, anarchists and revolutionaries assassinated the Presidents of France and Italy, the Kings of Portugal and Italy, the Prime Minister of Spain, the Empress of Austria, and there were attempts on the German Kaiser and Chancellor. Queen Victoria survived eight assassination attempts. The targets of anarchists and revolutionaries were almost always government officials, rather than members of the public.

Over the years, a great many heads of state or government have been assassinated. They are listed at Appendix B. Also listed are political assassinations, those who survived assassinations, suspicious deaths and known assassins.

The term assassin is probably derived from the Arabic word hashshishiyyin, meaning hashish. It is believed that the founder of the Assassins, Hasan-e Sabbah used hashish to motivate his sect members to undertake assassinations. The hashish connection reportedly led to the group becoming known as the Assassins.

Webster's dictionary defines assassination as 'To murder by guile or by sudden violence'. According to *Black's Law Dictionary* assassination is 'Murder committed for hire. A murder committed treacherously by stealth or surprise, or by lying in wait'. The *Macquarie Dictionary* defines assassination as 'killing by sudden or secret, premeditated assault, especially for political or religious motives'.

Both terrorists and states conduct political assassinations but assassination is a politically loaded term suggesting illegality. Israel therefore refers to its assassinations of Palestinians as 'targeted killings'. The moral equivalence argument is that it is no more acceptable for a state to engage in murder than it is for a terrorist to do so.

In a war situation, assassination of a military leader might shorten a war (for example, the targeting of Saddam Hussein), but it is a tactic that has not been used regularly in the past because it complicates dealings with a defeated enemy.

Execution of captured enemy leaders without fair trial is considered a war crime. Not preventing a war crime from being committed is complicity. It has been suggested that President Bush's resistance to making US military personnel liable to an international court process is motivated in part by the claims that have been made that US Special Forces personnel stood by while their Afghan allies killed Taliban prisoners.

The motive for assassination may be revenge or retaliation, to pre-empt a threat, to remove a problem individual, to disrupt a group, to deter, to cause change, or to demonstrate control or capability. Key aspects are surprise, premeditation, political motivation, stature of the target individual, and shock effect.

Terrorist groups will target politicians, senior military officers, judges, leading businesspeople, influential opposition figures within ethnic groups, and leaders of rival terrorist groups.

States will target terrorist leaders, terrorist bomb makers, sometimes (in the case of Israel) leaders of the political wing of a terrorist group, those seen as a threat to national security, and outspoken expatriates. States usually use their intelligence and security services, Special Forces, or hired criminals to conduct assassinations.

From a terrorist perspective, a state leader is a symbolic, high profile target of the adversary state. Assassination of a state or terrorist leader may cause substantial disruption, particularly where there is no clear successor. Fear of retaliation often deters state leaders from ordering the assassination of those who could respond in kind. One of the unpredictable factors for a terrorist group is that assassination of a state leader might have undesirable consequences. For example, Al Qaeda could target President Bush but may choose not to do so because in their view his responses are predictable and in their longer-term interest, whereas those of his successor may not be.

Terrorist groups may have a hit squad trained to carry out targeted hits, like the Sparrow Units of the New People's Army in the Philippines or the Provisional IRA's Active Service Units.

Those who might be responsible for assassinations, in addition to terrorists and states, include mentally unbalanced individuals, radical individuals, political rivals, or organised crime groups such as the Italian Mafia.

Assassination by a state

A state will hope that the assassination or removal of a prominent terrorist leader will have the effect of destroying the will of the group or causing the group to break up into factions that might be easier to deal with. The Kurdish PKK leader Abdullah Ocalan's arrest in February 1999 by Turkish special forces in Kenya led to a loss of will on the part of the PKK—although there were other reasons too for the PKK's reduction in violence.

The fortuitous, rather than planned, killing by the Philippines Police of the Abu Sayyaf Group leader Abdurajak Janjalani in December 1998 led to that group breaking up into localised factions.

In 1976, US President Ford issued an executive order banning US agencies from being involved in assassinations. Ford's main concern was retaliation against prominent Americans. Prior to that time CIA and other agencies were implicated in the deaths of (or attempts against) Cuban President Castro, Congolese Prime Minister Lumumba, Chilean President Allende, Dominican President Trujillo, revolutionary

Che Guevara, and many others. Since September 11, the United States has resumed assassinations, this time targeting known terrorist leaders, particularly the Al Qaeda leadership. An attempt was made to kill Osama bin Laden in August 1998 using Tomahawk missiles, and Mohammed Atef, the Al Qaeda operations chief, was killed by USAF aerial bombing in October 2001. There have been reports that Osama bin Laden was wounded at Tora Bora in November or December 2001.

The controversial US Army School of the Americas (SOA) (now known as the Western Hemisphere Institute for Security Cooperation) at Fort Benning, Georgia continued to train individuals from Latin America in assassination techniques throughout the 1990s. Its graduates include many notorious Latin American dictators. Critics of the SOA sometimes referred to it as 'The School of the Assassins'.

States that have been known to conduct assassinations in the past are Israel, North Korea, Russia, and the United States.

Israel is still involved on an ongoing basis in the assassination of Palestinian extremists. Numerous Palestinian terrorists and political leaders have been assassinated since the 1970s, mainly by Israeli undercover intelligence operatives and missiles launched from helicopters.

In 1996, Chechen terrorist leader Dzhokar Dudayev was killed by a Russian missile that homed in on his satellite phone. A recent example of state assassination is the killing of the Al Qaeda warlord, Khattab, who was poisoned by the Russian FSB in Chechnya in 2002.

Several Al Qaeda operatives have been killed by the United States since September 11, mainly through aircraft strikes and missiles directed from unmanned aerial vehicles (UAVs). One example is Abu al-Harithi, one of the USS *Cole* attack planners, who was killed in Yemen in November 2002 by Hellfire missiles launched from a Predator UAV.

One of the possible outcomes of assassination of a key terrorist is that the problem goes away. It may however result in instability, disruption, tighter group security, and a new, more ruthless, leader coming forward. Or, in the absence of another clear leader, there may be several leadership candidates and a fragmentation of the group into factions that could be less predictable and therefore more of a problem. Any assassination gains may be short term because there will usually be retaliation and continuation of the cycle of violence. (Israel provides the best example of this syndrome.)

Vulnerability to assassination attempts

Leaders of Western states and governments are vulnerable to terrorist assassination for a number of reasons. These include that their travel routes and program are publicly known in advance and they are expected to be accessible to the public. Suicide attackers have a good chance of breaching close personal protection (CPP) defences. Specialist weapons provide a stand-off assassination capability (.50 cal sniper rifles have a range of 2000 metres, while some surface to air missiles are effective to 15,000 feet). It is far more difficult to assassinate autocratic leaders like Saddam Hussein because they rarely announce their public appearances beforehand and may employ body-doubles to enhance their security.

Some venues where Western leaders are to speak need to be booked a long way ahead, creating a significant security problem. For example, political party conference venues need to be booked months or even years beforehand, allowing terrorists to build bombs into hotel VIP suites or other areas for later detonation. In October 1984, Prime Minister Margaret Thatcher's cabinet narrowly escaped a PIRA bomb at the Grand Hotel in Brighton during the Conservative Party's annual conference. Patrick Joseph Magee hid a bomb in September 1984 behind a panel in room 629. It comprised a long delay timer and 11 kilograms of high explosive. It detonated in the early morning hours of 12 October, bringing down the chimneystack which fell through several floors, killing five prominent members of the Conservative Party and injuring 30.

There was concern about the Spanish King's security before the Barcelona Olympics when faint beeping was heard in the King's box. After sound-locating equipment was brought in, the sound was traced to one of the concrete walls. The wall was demolished and the cause turned out to be a digital Casio watch (nearly always the terrorist watch of choice for bombs) that a worker had accidentally dropped into the cement as it was being poured. The beeping was the battery running down! It could however just as easily have been a bomb left in the cement for later detonation.

For their part, terrorist leaders are vulnerable too, because the leadership function inevitably means holding meetings and using mobile phones, both of which provide states with targeting opportunities. States are also in a position to handsomely reimburse informants and provide protection programs for defectors.

CHAPTER ELEVEN

MACROTERRORISM

My definition of macroterrorism is 'An act of terrorism that is substantially greater than the norm in its effect on a target population'. (Possible outcomes include unusually high loss of life, major property damage or economic loss, and/or destruction of a national iconic structure.)

The aim of such an act might be to undermine the credibility of a state (or states) and its leadership, to dislocate the international 'system', to cause a polarisation of ethnic or religious groups, to escalate from 'normal' level terrorist attacks, to seek revenge against society, to debilitate an adversary, or to create a situation of national or international instability.

What could cause an act of macroterrorism? There are several options: use of chemical, biological, radiological or nuclear (CBRN) weapons; cyberterrorism; and conventional 'low-tech high-impact' attacks (such as the September 11 attacks). A newer term is 'CBRNE'—the 'E' includes the effects of a very large conventional explosive device.

No currently active terrorist group is known to have CBRN weapons. Al Qaeda *may* however have small quantities of chemical and biological agents. Al Qaeda also knows theoretically how to construct nuclear and radiological weapons, and it is possible—but very unlikely—that Al Qaeda has Spetsnaz (Russian Special Forces) tactical nuclear weapons.

It is doubtful that any state sponsor would provide CBRN weapons to a terrorist group, or knowingly allow terrorist construction of CBRN weapons on its territory.

An exception might be a state with its back to the wall and nothing to lose, such as Iraq if it had had weapons of mass destruction just before or during Operation Iraqi Freedom, or North Korea if it believed it was facing imminent US attack.

Many states have been guilty of state macroterrorism in the past. The best known recent example is the Iraqi use of chemical bombs against the Kurds at Halabja, in March 1988, which killed between several hundred and perhaps as many as 5000 civilians. (The evidence available is very subjective.)

Use of chemical agents

Chemical agents are manufactured and inanimate, and categorised as either: blister agents, choking agents, nerve agents, blood agents, or incapacitating agents.

The most deadly terrorist attack to date using a chemical agent was Aum Shinrikyo's sarin gas attack on the Tokyo subway system in March 1995, which killed 12 people and injured 5500.

Toxic chemical agents that could be used by terrorists to cause casualties include hydrogen cyanide and some industrial chemicals (Al Qaeda has probably experimented with hydrogen cyanide—there is a video on the Internet showing a chemical agent, believed to be hydrogen cyanide (but it could possibly be sarin) being tested on a dog at an Al Qaeda camp in Afghanistan). Toxic chemical agents are of course available in the industrial areas of cities. Combining a conventional bomb with a vehicle carrying hazardous materials, such as petroleum products, could also produce a dangerous contamination and health hazard.

Use of biological agents

The second category—biological agents, or bioagents, comprise pathogens that cause disease in man, such as bacteria, rickettsiae (transmitted by the bite of ticks, lice and fleas), and viruses; and toxins. Bacteria-derived agents include anthrax, bubonic plague, pneumonic plague, tularaemia or rabbit fever, meningitis, typhoid fever, and dysentery. If not treated quickly they often cause death. Viruses require a living host and are sub-microscopic and as a result can pass through filter systems that would collect bacteria and rickettsiae. There is often no available treatment. Toxins attack the nervous system. They are non-living poisons that can be derived from animals, plants or marine algae. A very lethal plant toxin is ricin, derived from the castor bean. Another is fentanyl—a powerful opiate. Toxins could also be disseminated in water supplies.

Biological agents can usually reproduce themselves, which means that you can produce large quantities with the right equipment. There is enormous potential for future advances in biotechnology and genetic engineering to make biological agents more predictable and more lethal.

Bacteria, viruses and other live agents may reproduce and transform once released into the environment, and may become more dangerous over time. Biological agents can however be difficult to prepare and use as weapons. Important variables for use can include the spore size and weather conditions. (Aum Shinrikyo was initially attracted to the use of anthrax, but gave up after several disseminations in public places failed to cause any casualties.)

The best-known recent biological agent incidents were the anthrax attacks in the United States that occurred after September 11, resulting in five deaths, believed to be the work of an individual who had at some time had access to US lab supplies of anthrax. (Anthrax is very durable and has a long shelf life.) These incidents were hoaxed throughout the world by copycat mischief-makers. It has recently been announced that the clean-up after the US attacks cost US$5 billion.

Since then there have been a number of reports that terrorists intend to use ricin (which like anthrax can be in white powder form), in terrorist attacks; the most deadly option would be to use it to contaminate foodstuffs.

Bacteria are easier for terrorists to cultivate than viruses, but there is the potential in the future to engineer infectious organisms, such as the hantaviruses; haemorrhagic fever (excessive bleeding) causing agents, such as Ebola, and the bacteria-invasive Group A streptococcus (commonly known as flesh-eating bacteria), to achieve more devastating effects. Other recent developments that could make biological attacks more deadly are the Australian re-engineering of harmless mousepox so that it now kills, and making viruses resistant to antibiotics. The artificial creation of the polio virus, while something of a stunt, could have long term implications for the manufacturing of more complex viruses, such as smallpox.

No consistently reliable field detection systems for bioagents are currently available, nor are bioagents recognisable to human senses.

The good news is that highly contagious bioagents are less likely to be used by Muslim extremists where there are adjacent Muslim countries because of the unpredictable 'blow-back' factor on unprotected Muslim populations. Non-contagious agents may be a more attractive option for terrorist use in most circumstances. (An apocalyptic cult or unbalanced individual might however have a different view.)

Use of radiological or nuclear weapons

Nuclear and radiological weapons include nuclear weapons, and weapons grade and non-weapons grade radioactive material. The most desirable option for a terrorist group would be the acquisition of an operational tactical nuclear weapon which could cause sufficient damage to destroy most Western cities. The most likely places that such a weapon might be obtained are the former Soviet Union or Pakistan.

There have been at least 10 known cases of attempted smuggling of radioactive material, with quantities increasing but insufficient to construct a warhead—and no confirmed cases so far of smuggling of a nuclear weapon. However, Russian stocks of non-fissile and fissile radioactive material are estimated at up to 300,000 tons and are vulnerable to criminal acquisition. The guards in Russia and the Ukraine are poorly paid and there is little doubt that the Russian mafia could obtain both nuclear material if it wanted to for terrorists. It may of course judge that it is not in its interest to be responsible for a nuclear attack in the United States—no matter how large the profit.

Nuclear materials are divided into two categories:

- Fissile material, such as plutonium—Pu-239 and highly enriched uranium (HEU)—U-235. (These are the best known options for making a nuclear explosive device.)
- Non-fissile radioactive material, such as Uranium 238 (used in nuclear reactors), Caesium 137 (used by steel fabricators), Cobalt 60 (cancer hospitals), Iodine 128 (hospitals), and Strontium 90 (hospital waste).

Weapons grade and non-weapons grade material is potentially available on the illegal arms market, and could find its way into criminal and terrorist hands in the future.

The only practical option for terrorists wanting to make a nuclear explosive device would be HEU, because construction of an HEU device is not particularly difficult once sufficient HEU has been obtained. (A plutonium-based nuclear device would be beyond even most states' capabilities.)

The main challenge for terrorists would be in obtaining the 15 to 30 kilograms of HEU needed to construct a workable device that would be sufficient to destroy an entire city. (Experts differ on how much would be needed.) Even 30 kilograms of HUE is not a lot of mass—it would fit into two and a half one-litre milk cartons. The most likely source would be the former Soviet Union's stockpile. (HEU can be hand-carried without significant radiation risk.)

A terrorist-constructed primitive nuclear device would not be a movable weapon and would have to be detonated in-place. Clandestine construction of such a device in a rented apartment or garage could be achieved by non-experts in a matter of weeks to months. It could then be detonated by remote control or a timer. The device's explosive yield would be unpredictable, but would probably be comparable to the

Hiroshima bomb—which was equivalent to about 20,000 tons of TNT. Potential human casualties would run into millions, and damage would run into trillions of US dollars.

The simplest 'nuclear' option would be a dirty bomb—a conventional explosive device used to disperse non-fissile radioactive material. This approach could be used to contaminate a large area using low-grade radioactive material, such as Caesium 137, or Cobalt 60.

Other forms of attack

We have already looked at cyberterrorism in Chapter 8. In relation to macroterrorism, the main concerns are physical violence against the information system of a target entity (potentially causing enormous economic loss) and cyberattack against the infrastructure of a target entity (that could also cause substantial loss of life). Terrorist groups have not yet moved beyond the first category cited (physical violence)—examples being the London financial district bomb attacks by the Provisional IRA on the Baltic Exchange in April 1992, and Bishopsgate in April 1993.

Major conventional attacks are the last area of concern. The enormous damage and casualties caused by the accidents at Bhopal and Chernobyl demonstrate the level of destruction that could be achieved by terrorists if they were to engineer such an event, perhaps by using an insider.

The poisonous gas leak from the Union Carbide plant at Bhopal in December 1984 killed more than 4000 people. Over 40 tonnes of highly poisonous methylisocyanate gas leaked out of the pesticide factory. At least 10,000 people have died since then, and ten more are dying every month due to exposure-related diseases.

In April 1986, the Chernobyl nuclear meltdown resulted in 31 deaths, but it is estimated that 6500 people may eventually die from cancers caused by the accident. Around 23% of the Ukraine is expected to remain contaminated for 130 years. Older plants that lack containment structures or modern safety features are a particular risk for similar types of accident or terrorist attack.

In terms of scenarios for causing mass casualties and major damage, there are literally hundreds of options available to terrorists. These options can be increased through organised crime connections.

Some maritime options could include: use of a merchant ship as a weapon (perhaps against a warship, bridge, pipeline, or oil or gas platform); use of a ship to deploy a weapon of mass destruction into a port city; use of a vessel to introduce economy-threatening diseases to food stocks, both onshore and offshore; and the use of a shipping container packed with conventional explosive, or containing a CBRN weapon.

Since the initiative lies with terrorists, it seems inevitable that there will be future acts of macroterrorism. Such attacks could affect several neighbouring states, or even possibly have a global impact.

To deal with them we will need well-practised multilateral emergency procedures to limit the effectiveness of macroterrorism attacks. It is clearly difficult to guard against all eventualities, but we are gradually putting safeguards into place.

Who then should we be looking at as possible macroterrorism perpetrators? The obvious contenders are a religiously motivated terrorist group like Al Qaeda, a rogue state, an unbalanced individual, or an apocalyptic cult.

CHAPTER TWELVE

COUNTERTERRORISM AND RISK MANAGEMENT

The need for effective counterterrorism measures became more apparent in western Europe following the terrorist attack at the 1972 Olympics. Palestinian terrorists broke into the Olympic village in Munich, killed two Israeli athletes immediately, and took another nine hostage. The Palestinians were seeking the release of 200 prisoners who were in jail in Israel. In a disastrous rescue attempt, Bavarian Police opened fire on the Palestinians at Munich airport, killing three of the Palestinians. In the ensuing battle, all nine athletes, two other Palestinians and a policeman were killed.

In counterterrorism, it is more important to look at longer-term solutions rather than just short-term violent solutions of the 'eye for an eye' type, as currently practised by the Israelis. The problem with a cycle of violence is that both sides soon lose sight of who started the cycle.

In the Palestinian context the Israelis are seeking revenge for the attacks on their forces, civilians, and settlers, while the Palestinians are attacking because of Israeli repression and Israel's illegal occupation of the West Bank and Gaza Strip. A strategic resolution involves consideration of root causes, which may include political factors such as discrimination, long-held grievances and injustices, and frustration over lack of change.

Long-term resolution is less of a priority for many government agencies because they benefit financially from fighting terrorism at a tactical level. Since September 11, all government agencies that have a role to play in safeguarding homeland security have received increased funding and resources to counter terrorism. Resolving terrorism, longer term, confers no institutional benefits and might well put bureaucrats out of a job. Churchill is reputed to have said that politicians look to the next election, while statesmen look to the next generation. Unfortunately the terrorism problem of the 21st century has not yet produced any visionaries, although Britain's Prime Minister Tony Blair has recognised that resolution of the Middle East's problems is a fundamental longer-term requirement. On the other hand, US strategic policy tends to work in four-year presidential cycles.

Tactical, or shorter term, measures include *defensive* counterterrorism (sometimes referred to as antiterrorism) measures (such as security-related legislation, upgraded protective security, tightened border security), and tactical *offensive* counterterrorism measures (such as intelligence activities, police investigations, and military operations).

An important element in any counterterrorism campaign is to undermine the terrorists' cause, isolating them from their constituency as far as possible. This can be achieved by:

- undermining their popular platform
- harassment and interdiction, and
- discrediting their political and military leadership.

An example of undermining would be granting greater autonomy to a separatist group, thereby satisfying the political element of the group and the majority of its supporters, and isolating the hard core independence elements. As an example, the Spanish government has successfully isolated ETA by granting more autonomy to the Basques.

On the harassment and interdiction front, the CIA monitored Egyptian terrorist leaders living in Albania and, when the Albanian government lost control of the country, the Egyptians were spirited out and returned to Egypt for trial. This kind of monitoring and arrest activity has made it difficult for Egypt's two major terrorist groups to mount a terrorism campaign in recent years.

Successful discrediting of the leadership is demonstrated by the case of Abdullah Ocalan and the Kurdish PKK. After PKK leader Ocalan was arrested by the Turks in February 1999, he started to cooperate to save himself from a death sentence, embarrassing those who had been prepared to die for the cause, and discrediting the PKK leadership in the eyes of many of its followers.

Many Muslim groups cite the plight of the Palestinians, and the United States' unqualified support for Israeli actions against the Palestinians, as their main complaint against the United States, but there are a number of other reasons for Muslim anger against the West and against many Muslim rulers. Some of the heat could certainly be taken out of the Palestinian issue by the United States pressuring Israel to honour international agreements and engage in meaningful dialogue with the Palestinians.[28]

Other measures that the West could work on include:

- avoidance of double standards in international politics
- a commitment to fair solutions for Middle East problems
- a better understanding of Islam
- encouragment of societal reforms in the Middle East
- removing incentives to use terrorism, through dialogue and having 'neutral' countries act as honest brokers in ethnonationalist conflicts (Norway has already been actively doing this)
- encouragement of non-violence, and
- offering alternative lifestyle options to Muslim youth.

In the ongoing fight against terrorism, intelligence is a key factor for success. Effectively countering terrorists involves the use of imagery intelligence (imint), signals intelligence (sigint), human intelligence (humint), open source intelligence (osint), security intelligence, and police intelligence, as well as intelligence from other key government national security agencies, such as Immigration and Customs. These products need to be fused as part of a national security or homeland security process.

Imagery intelligence can provide information on terrorist training areas and allows after-attack examination of ground activities to see who was responsible. In one case, it was possible to backtrack a Palestinian terrorist support vessel on satellite imagery to its start point in Libya.

Signals intelligence facilitates the monitoring of terrorist communications, including all types of phones and faxes, as well as the Internet. Even if the communications cannot be broken or decrypted, an increase in communications activity can be an indicator of pending operational activity.

Human intelligence can give you inside information on what a terrorist group is planning. The Israelis are well informed on what is happening within extremist movements in the West Bank and the Gaza Strip and will exploit available pressure points. For example, it is difficult for Palestinian tertiary students to get permission from the Israelis to travel abroad unless they agree in writing to cooperate on their return.

Open source intelligence provides access to information that terrorists could also be accessing and provides information about what they could be planning, for example, how they might plan to construct a dirty bomb or how they might try to attack a target based on publicly available information. The main sources of such information are the Internet, the media and public information sources, such as libraries.

Security intelligence provides information on ways in which terrorists are trying to breach security systems, who the key members of activist groups are, what demonstrations and operations are planned and what links exist between groups.

Police intelligence can provide information on contact between terrorists and criminals, while other government agencies (such as Immigration and Customs) can provide information that might be relevant to the overall threat assessment process.

Attempts to profile terrorists (including for extra attention at security screening points) have been unsuccessful to date. Even if you decide that a particular nationality should get greater attention, such as Pakistanis or

Saudis, terrorists will form only a tiny minority from that group. What you can do at a screening point is not waste time screening those who are highly unlikely to be a potential problem, such as the elderly, or children under the age of 15.

There are of course many other applications of these different types of intelligence to terrorism. The examples above are the tip of the iceberg. An intelligence collection plan would normally involve the use of a combination of sources to address a particular information requirement.

Technical means, such as audio monitoring devices, surveillance devices, vehicle tracking devices, and UAVs also have important intelligence applications.

National authorities need to try to stay one step ahead through intelligence sharing and cooperation, conducting security threat analyses to better understand the nature of the threat, adoption of risk management strategies to make best use of available resources, and undertaking intelligence 'estimates' (up to five years into the future) and 'forecasts' (five years plus). Terrorism may be forecasted to change, for example, based on changing demographics that can be anticipated 10 to 20 years ahead.

Tactical operations can include the conduct of aggressive assassination operations, some of which were addressed in the previous chapter. One example was the November 2002 assassination attack by the United States in Yemen. The CIA targeted a car containing six suspected Al Qaeda members, including one of the suspected planners of the attack on the USS *Cole* in October 2000. Hellfire missiles were launched from a UAV, destroying the car and killing its occupants.

Israel has a long record of assassinations. These include the October 1995 killing of Fathi Shiqaqi, leader of Palestine Islamic Jihad (PIJ), in Malta; the January 1996 killing of Yahya Ayyash, one of the chief bomb-makers for Hamas; and the September 1997 botched assassination attempt against Khaled Meshal, political chief of Hamas in Jordan.

In the latter case, the Mossad agents were arrested in Jordan, despite an undertaking that Mossad would not act on Jordanian soil. They were also carrying Canadian passports despite another undertaking, given to

Canada following a previous incident, that they would not do so. The Mossad agents had applied a toxic gas to Meshal's neck. Following the political storm that erupted between Jordan and Israel, the Israelis were reportedly forced to reveal the poison used so that the Jordanians could provide the antidote to Meshal, and the Israelis agreed to release Sheikh Ahmed Yassin, the late spiritual leader of Hamas and PIJ.

Since the start of the latest intifada in September 2000, the Israelis have relied more on the use of air to surface missiles (ASMs) for the destruction of vehicles believed to be carrying terrorists. These are euphemistically referred to as 'targeted killings'.

While assassination may create short-term gratification for the state that is targeting a terrorist organisation, and may result in some disruption to a terrorist organisation's activities, there is no evidence that assassination produces any lasting effects. On the contrary, it seems to perpetuate the conflict. The conflict between the Israelis and the Palestinians has not diminished over the years, despite the number of assassinations, because the Palestinians' grievances remain unresolved. If anything, their opposition is now more intense than it was in the past.

Some of the ways that security can be enhanced in government and industry include: having a security awareness program, compartmentalising information (so that individual employees and other organisations only have access to the information they need), having physical barriers for infrastructure protection, screening suspect mail, practising evacuation and emergency procedures, having a high standard of IT security, conducting security vetting of staff, and vetting aftercare (regular reviewing of clearances), and maintaining high security standards.

Different industries will have different security requirements. Airport and airline options, for example, include effective airport perimeter security, security vetting of staff, air-side access controls, screening of passengers, screening of baggage, removal of hand-held items from aircraft at transit stops, use of bomb resistant cargo containers, and use of explosives detectors. One of the security problems faced by airports is the high turnover rate of casual air-side staff, who have access to planes and their cargo.

Counterterrorism units

Most countries have counterterrorism (CT) forces on-call at all times, drawn from the armed forces, gendarmeries or other paramilitary groups, national police, or regional police. The response of the United Kingdom or Australia to a terrorist incident would involve the deployment of regular law enforcement officers, specialist SWAT police, then the SAS.

Some Western CT units include:

- Germany—GSG-9 (formed in 1973, in response to the Munich Olympics, from the Border Guards);
- United Kingdom—Special Air Services or SAS (formed from the British army early in World War II);
- United States—FBI (responsible for counterterrorism armed response in the United States), US Army Delta Force (formed in the 1970s and operating outside the continental United States), the US Navy Special Warfare Development Group (Dev Group) (also operating outside the continental United States))
- France—Groupe D'lntervention Gendarmerie Nationale (GIGN or National Gendarmerie, formed in 1974).

Many Asian forces are modelled on, or have been trained by, the UK SAS, the German GSG-9, and the US military or FBI. They include:

- India—Marine Commando (Marcos) units
- Indonesia—Detachment 81 of Kopassus (Army), Den Bravo (Air Force), Detachment 88 (Police)
- Japan—police SWAT teams
- South Korea—707th Special Mission Battalion
- Taiwan—Police, Military Police, Special Service Forces (Marines).

Other lesser known CT units include: Israeli Sayeret Mat'kal; Dutch Marine BBE; Belgian Gendarmerie Diane; Austrian Gendarmerie Cobra; Spanish Civil Guard UEI; Italian Carabinieri GIS; French

Police RAID; Italian Police NOCS; Spanish Police GEO; and Israeli Police Ya'ma'm.

Response to aircraft hijackings

From the 1970s, one of the major challenges for CT forces became politically motivated aircraft hijackings. Some of the more noteworthy incidents are described below.

In July 1976 at Entebbe in Uganda, Israeli commandos ended a week-long hijacking of an Air France airliner by Palestinian and German terrorists. The terrorists had already released the non-Jewish and non-Israeli passengers. The remaining Jewish and Israeli passengers were rescued while seven terrorists were killed as well as 20 Ugandan soldiers. One Israeli officer and four Israeli civilians were killed, including one Israeli woman who was left behind in a Ugandan hospital and disappeared, murdered by the Ugandan authorities on the orders of dictator Idi Amin.

In October 1977, four members of the Popular Front for the Liberation of Palestine (PFLP), demanding the release of jailed comrades, held a German Lufthansa airliner on the ground at Mogadishu, Somalia, and killed the captain. The German GSG-9 with UK SAS assistance stormed the plane and freed 87 hostages. Only one hijacker, a woman, survived.

Response to other siege situations

There have been other notable siege hostage situations, other than those involving aircraft.

In January 1980 in Guatemala peasant, labour and student activists peacefully took over the Spanish Embassy to protest against the government of General Fernando Romeo Lucas Garcia. The government refused to negotiate and stormed the embassy, setting fire to it. Almost 40 activists and embassy staff were burned to death.

In April 1980 in Iran, eight US servicemen on counterterrorism operation, Eagle Claw, died when a helicopter and transport plane collided and burst into flames at 'Desert One', a rendezvous in the desert of south-eastern Iran. The operation had been mounted by the Carter administration to free 52 American Embassy hostages held in Tehran since the Iranian revolution the year before. The operation had to be aborted.

In November 1985, in Colombia, M-19 guerrillas occupied the Justice Palace in Bogota to protest what they termed a betrayal by President Belisario Betancur in peace talks. The Colombian Army attacked, killing about 100 people, including 11 Supreme Court justices.

Also in November 1985, at Malta, Egyptian 777 commandos attempted to rescue EgyptAir passengers after the three Abu Nidal Organisation hijackers started killing US and Israeli passengers. 61 people died before or during the rescue attempt—as well as two of the three hijackers.

In January 1996 in Russia, Chechen rebels seized a hospital in Dagestan, a republic bordering Chechnya, and took more than 100 hostages. Russian forces launched a four-day bombardment of the Dagestan village where the hostages were being held. Dozens of hostages were killed but most of the rebels escaped.

In April 1997 in Peru, troops stormed the Japanese ambassador's mansion, freeing dozens of hostages held by Tupac Amaru Revolutionary Movement (MRTA) terrorists for four months, killing all 14 of the MRTA captors. There have since been allegations, probably true, of the deliberate execution of some MRTA members by the security forces, after they were captured alive.

In August 2000 in Sierra Leone, a British patrol comprising 11 soldiers from the Royal Irish Regiment and one Sierra Leonean soldier was seized by renegades known as the West Side Boys, near Masiaka, 100 km east of the capital, Freetown. Five of the most junior soldiers were released in exchange for a generator and satellite phone. There were fears that the others would be executed after negotiations broke down.

On 10 September 2000, Operation Barras was launched and 150 British paratroopers, brought in secretly from the United Kingdom, stormed the camp in an early morning raid supported by the SAS. The hostages were rescued and 25 of the West Side Boys were killed with many more captured, including the leader, 'Brigadier' Foday Kallay. A British commando was killed, one paratrooper was seriously wounded and a number of others were lightly wounded. The operation was judged a great success because of the degree of difficulty and possibility that the West Side Boys planned to execute the hostages.

On 26 October 2002, Russian Special Forces stormed a Moscow theatre where about 50 Chechen rebels were holding more than 800 hostages. The Chechens had made demands for a Russian withdrawal from Chechnya and had wired up the theatre with explosives. After three days, Russian authorities pumped gas into the theatre before mounting an assault. Almost all of the 124 hostages who died were killed by gas inhalation. Russian security forces executed all of the Chechens.

The Russian authorities were evasive about the gas used but speculation has centred on fentanyl, an opiate, which has a similar effect to an anaesthetic, and BZ, an LSD-like agent that the United States developed in the 1960s to cause disorientation. The Russian authorities have never revealed the full truth of the attack which, while supported by President Bush for political reasons, ranks high among incompetent rescues of hostages.

It is obviously very important to know the motivation of terrorists before trying to resolve a situation by force. Muslim extremists are more likely to be prepared to sacrifice themselves, while terrorists with a separatist agenda are more likely to negotiate.

International Conventions on Counterterrorism

There are 13 international conventions underlining the international approach to countering terrorism. Cooperative measures have received new impetus since September 11. As noted earlier, states are required to ensure that their legislation is in line with conventions they have ratified.

The UN terrorism-related conventions are:[29]

- The Convention on Offences and Certain Other Acts Committed on Board Aircraft (Tokyo, Japan in 1963)
- The Convention for the Suppression of Unlawful Seizure of Aircraft (The Hague, the Netherlands in 1970)
- The Convention for the Suppression of Unlawful Acts Against the Safety of Civil Aviation (Montreal, Canada in 1971)
- The Convention on the Prevention and Punishment of Crimes Against Internationally Protected Persons, including Diplomatic Agents (New York, USA in 1973)
- The International Convention Against the Taking of Hostages (New York, USA in 1979)
- The Convention on the Physical Protection of Nuclear Material (Vienna, Austria in 1980)
- The Protocol for the Suppression of Unlawful Acts of Violence at Airports Serving International Civil Aviation—Supplementary to the 1971 Montreal Convention (Montreal, Canada in 1988)
- The Convention for the Suppression of Unlawful Acts Against the Safety of Maritime Navigation (Rome, Italy in 1988)
- The Protocol for the Suppression of Unlawful Acts Against the Safety of Fixed Platforms Located in the Continental Shelf (Rome, Italy in 1988)
- The Convention on the Marking of Plastic Explosives for the Purpose of Detection (also known as the Marplex Convention) (Montreal, Canada in 1991)
- The Convention on the Suppression of Terrorist Bombings (New York, USA in 1997)
- The Convention for the Suppression of the Financing of Terrorism (New York, USA in 1999)
- Draft Convention for the Suppression of Acts of Nuclear Terrorism (Under negotiation in New York).

Significant regional conventions include:

- Convention to Prevent and Punish Acts of Terrorism Taking the

Form of Crimes against Persons and Related Extortion that are of International Significance, concluded in Washington DC, USA on 2 February 1971.

- European Convention on the Suppression of Terrorism, concluded at Strasbourg, France on 27 January 1977.
- SAARC Regional Convention on Suppression of Terrorism, signed at Katmandu, Nepal on 4 November 1987.
- Arab Convention on the Suppression of Terrorism, signed at a meeting held at the General Secretariat of the League of Arab States in Cairo, Egypt on 22 April 1998.
- Treaty on Cooperation among the States Members of the Commonwealth of Independent States in Combating Terrorism, signed at Minsk, Belarus on 4 June 1999.
- Convention of the Organisation of the Islamic Conference on Combating International Terrorism, adopted at Ouagadougou, Burkina Faso on 1 July 1999.
- OAU Convention on the Prevention and Combating of Terrorism, adopted at Algiers, Algeria on 14 July 1999.

Retaliatory attacks

The US-led attack on Afghanistan in October 2001 and Iraq in March 2003 emphasised a longstanding United States belief that states have a right to retaliate against other states that have sponsored terrorism against them. The US-led attack on Afghanistan was generally viewed as justified by the September 11 attacks, but the April 2003 pre-emptive attack on Iraq was seen by most states as unwarranted since Iraq did not pose a credible threat to the United States. The Bush administration's view is that the United States has the right to pre-emptively attack any state that poses a potential threat to the United States.

The United States has however pursued a retaliatory policy for many years. Some of the occasions are listed below.

In April 1986, in West Berlin, two US soldiers and a Turkish woman were killed in the bombing of the La Belle disco, which was popular with US soldiers. Another 153 were wounded, including 49 US servicemen. The attack was linked to Libya. President Reagan authorised Operation El Dorado Canyon and, nine days later, US aircraft bombed Tripoli, killing 37 people, including the adopted daughter of Libyan President Colonel Moamar Gaddafi.

In April 1993, President Clinton authorised the launching of Tomahawk cruise missiles against the Iraqi intelligence service headquarters because of 'compelling evidence' that Baghdad had plotted to assassinate former president George Bush during a visit to Kuwait.

On 20 August 1998, following the Al Qaeda bombing on 7 August 1998 of two US embassies in Nairobi, Kenya and Dar es Salaam, Tanzania, the United States launched 80 cruise missiles against the Al-Shifa pharmaceutical plant in Khartoum in the Sudan and six sites in Afghanistan. (One of the outcomes of the attack was the recovery by Pakistan of at least two Tomahawk missiles that had not detonated and the loss of Tomahawk cruise missile technology to China.)

Counterterrorism and policing

From a police perspective, a key aspect to dealing effectively with terrorism is having good intelligence. Law enforcement personnel have a range of sources not available to other security and intelligence agencies. These include informants, information obtained through routine policing, and information from jail populations. Members of the public are also more likely to give information to community based police than they are to security agencies because police are usually more accessible to the public. In the United States both security and national policing functions are combined in the FBI, which should mean that it is aware of local security issues, although this seems not to have been the case before September 11. To be more accessible to the public, many countries, including Australia, now have free-call national security hotlines, and these have proved to be a useful additional option for obtaining information.

Other policing aspects of counterterrorism are keeping pressure on wanted terrorists and their supporters and disrupting their operations through active investigations, allowing no statute of limitations for terrorism offences, having an aggressive arrest policy, and legislation that allows protracted interviewing of persons believed to be involved in terrorism.

Examples of proactive policing are provided by the Ramzi Yousef and Mir Kasi cases.

Ramzi Ahmed Yousef, a Muslim extremist with an Iraqi passport, was indicted in 1993 on charges of taking part in the first World Trade Center bombing in February 1993, along with four others who were convicted in 1994. Yousef was one of the world's most wanted fugitives with a $US2 million bounty on his head for the attack. He was captured in Islamabad, Pakistan in February 1995 and returned to the United States. Prosecutors said he had left the United States on the day of the bombing. When he was convicted in a US court, he was sentenced to life plus 240 years in prison, without chance of parole.

On 25 January 1993, Mir Aimal Kasi sprayed AK-47 assault rifle fire into cars waiting to turn into the CIA's main gate at Langley, Virginia. Two CIA staff were killed. Three others were wounded. Kasi fled to Pakistan a day after the shootings. He was captured in Quetta, Pakistan by FBI agents and Pakistan police in June 1997, and confessed to the attack on the flight back to the United States. He was subsequently convicted, sentenced to death, and executed in Virginia in the United States. His body was returned to his family in Pakistan.

The FBI has been assisted in Pakistan by the police but their efforts are often undermined by the Inter Services Intelligence agency which has its own agenda.

Some other ways that counterterrorism measures can pressure terrorists is to increase public awareness, deny terrorists a safe-haven, place sanctions on sponsor states, block funds and fund raising, maintain an international list of banned terrorist organisations, and conduct active military operations where appropriate.

At a national level, important issues for the future are having an integrated homeland security approach, maintaining effective response measures to deal with any potential incident, using emerging countermeasure technologies effectively, adopting uniform international and national approaches, and knowing likely perpetrators' targeting preferences and methodologies.

Terrorism risk management

One aspect of counterterrorism looks at how to assess a security threat, manage the risk, and maintain business continuity.

A security threat assessment (STA) is an assessment of the security threat posed by one or more sources of risk. The level of a threat is derived from consideration of capability and intent.

When assessing a military threat, the usual unknown factor is 'intent'. You can readily determine what a potential adversary's military capability is through a range of intelligence sources, and assess what it might be in, say, five years time by reviewing its planned weapon purchases. The opposite is the case with terrorists—you know their intent, but knowing their capability is more problematic. They are not dependent on 'visible' capabilities, hence the US intelligence agencies' failure to assess correctly Al Qaeda's capability prior to September 11.

The STA is used by defence intelligence to provide information about the sources of potential threat and their likelihood. They must then be assessed to determine their potential to cause harm. The most likely sources of threat to most Western countries are politically motivated activists, politically motivated individuals, and terrorists. A possible format for a reasonably comprehensive overseas STA is included at Appendix C.

To return to risk factors, risk is exposure to an event that could result in loss or gain. Risk is measured in terms of event likelihood and consequences.[30] The management of risk involves identifying analysing, assessing, treating and monitoring risk.[31] People managing an activity must decide how to approach the activity to keep the risk within acceptable bounds, and decide what resources will be allocated to do so. There are five steps in the process:

- Prepare an STA, which will normally be specific to, for example, a particular group or industry. This involves gathering information and identifying the threat.
- Analyse the risks.
- Assess and prioritise the risks.
- Treat the risks (and prepare the security plan).
- Monitor the risk environment and evaluate the security plan.

Types of risk arising from politically motivated violence can include assassination, sabotage, civil unrest, riots, demonstrations, hostage situations, hijacking, bombings and armed attack.

The risk level is determined by rating the likelihood and consequence of action in accordance with the Australian 4360 Standard. Likelihoods are rated: Almost Certain, Likely, Moderate, Unlikely, Rare. Consequences are rated: Extreme, Very High, Medium, Low and Negligible. By combining these two in a matrix you end up with a risk level at each intersection of Consequences and Likelihood or Severe, High, Major, Significant, Moderate, Low or Trivial. The process can also be used to identify potential exploitation opportunities. For example, a business that has planned ahead for terrorist disruption can benefit at the expense of its rivals if there is sector-wide disruption, for whatever reason.

Business continuity management may be defined as the maintenance of critical outputs when one or more key inputs are unavailable. All organisations need to be able to recover quickly from a politically motivated violent incident—or an extraordinary or unusual event that disrupts normal business.[32] Bombs and incendiary devices are weapons that would cause a major disruption to normal operations, but are more likely to affect operations overseas than domestically, for businesses based in most developed countries. More common are politically motivated demonstrations that can disrupt normal operations in a less violent way, for example, street marches with sit-ins, or targeted protests, like leftist May Day marches or anti-globalisation demonstrations.

CHAPTER THIRTEEN

THE OVERSEAS THREAT TO TRAVELLERS

There are of course many non-terrorism-related hazards associated with overseas travel—illness, crime and natural hazards being the most obvious ones. I have listed a few general points of advice in Appendix D—but travel advice today is worthy of a book in its own right.

Many parts of the Middle East, Africa and South America have high poverty levels, anger against the United States and the West for perceived injustices, and a weak capability to counter or contain terrorism. 'No-go areas' are common.

Backpackers are probably guilty of doing the least travel planning, despite the fact that they are often travelling through dangerous areas. The prudent traveller should always consult government travel advisory web sites before planning a trip. The UK, US, Canadian and Australian governments all maintain up-to-date travel advisories that allow you to compare their analysts' opinions.[33] Travel books, including the *Lonely Planet* series, also provide travel advice.[34] It is obviously prudent to have some understanding of the areas to be traversed and a smattering of the language if you are backpacking. If you are kidnapped, it at least shows you have some interest in the place and its people and it might help you to bond with the kidnappers and survive!

Data relating to Australian deaths from politically motivated violence (PMV) shows that most deaths occur overseas. In Australia's case, since 1900 there have been 160 deaths from PMV as of March 2004—22 in Australia and 138 overseas. While I do not have such accurate data for other countries, general reporting of PMV incidents suggests that this is probably true of most other Western countries—that is, a danger ratio of abroad to home of around 6:1. This would not be statistically true of the United States in 2001 because of the September 11 domestic death toll, but it probably holds true for most years other than 1995 (the Oklahoma bombing).

Tourists are particularly at risk because they provide a soft target for terrorists. And, typically, dangerous areas offer cheap deals to attract tourists.

Some foreigners have little choice but to work in dangerous locations—like non-government organisation (NGO) employees, UN peacekeepers and workers, and journalists. In Afghanistan, for example, Taliban and Al Qaeda remnants have particularly targeted these groups, killing a number of their personnel. The same has proved true of Iraq where international workers are seen as assisting the US occupiers.

Diplomats and embassies are also prime targets for terrorists. Countries that are likely to be targeted—notably the United States, Israel and the United Kingdom—have hardened their embassies and become even more security conscious.

High profile businesses that are identified with a target country are also at risk. The business most likely to be identified is the national airline of a targeted country or air carriers with the targeted country in their title. Because it was an easy way for Libya or Iran to get back at the United States, the US airline PanAm was targeted in 1988, resulting in the Lockerbie disaster. American Airlines was targeted by Richard Reid—the shoe bomber—presumably because it is an American airline. British Airways and Qantas face a threat because of their governments' well-known close association with the United States and identification with US strategic policies and the war on terror.

Richard Reid targeted an American Airlines flight out of Paris bound for Miami in December 2001. (According to aviation security experts, the first known 'shuicide' attack!) When Reid initially tried to board the flight out of Paris, the American Airlines check-in counter referred him back to the French border police for further examination. Suspicions were aroused by his having no hold baggage, having Arabic literature in his bag, and paying cash for a one-way ticket. The French police searched him, but did not look at his shoes. They ran the metal detecting wand over them, but his shoe bombs had been constructed without metal. The explosive was in the sole of the shoe and the black powder fuse was inside the shoes. It had to be lit once the shoe had been removed.

What the police did do though was to take away his gas lighter. This ultimately proved to be a critical factor. By the time the French police had finished checking him, Reid had missed his flight and American Airlines boarded him overnight at their expense in a hotel near the airport. The next morning, he was put on another American Airlines flight. During the course of this flight, he removed a shoe and attempted to light the fuse. However his matches had been hidden inside his shoes and had become damp from his sweat. When he tried to strike them, they just fizzled. He was soon accosted by the flight attendant and, when he struck her, was overpowered by an NBA basketball player fortuitously seated behind him.

Although this was an internal attack on an aircraft, the greatest danger faced by civil aircraft today is the use of a surface-to-air missile (SAM) against them. There is usually one such attack a year. More than 500 people have died from missile strikes on aircraft over the past ten years. Since they have been principally in Africa, Eastern Europe and Sri Lanka it has not aroused great concern elsewhere. The latest and best-known incident was the attempted take-down of an Israeli charter jet carrying Israeli tourists out of Mombasa, Kenya in November 2002.

The danger to an aircraft is greatest when take-off is in daylight hours. Within South-East Asia, aircraft leaving Bangkok are vulnerable to attacks of this kind because of the availability of SAMs in that part of Asia and because Al Qaeda's local affiliate, Jemaah Islamiah, is believed to have the intent to use them. Ground security at Bangkok is also poor. Elsewhere in the world, most African airports are high risk. Concerned travellers should think about the scheduling of their aircraft, and the desirability of passing through or departing from dangerous locations at night. Israel is now marketing an anti-missile system for civilian passenger aircraft.

Several years ago, I worked with Prakash Mirchandani (a former ABC journalist), Bushy Kavanagh (a former RAAF bush survival expert) and Graham Brammer OAM (a former SAS warrant officer) to provide survival training for work travellers. I was responsible for the security threat portion of the course. Prakash's view was that agencies that sent employees overseas had a duty of care to them, which should include showing them how to survive in dangerous circumstances. We ran several courses but the largest Australian departments (Defence and Foreign Affairs and Trade) did not send anyone to the courses. Unfortunately, it was an idea before its time. Had Prakash run the courses after September 11 and the Bali bombing, there would obviously have been much greater interest. As it was, by then Bushy had died of cancer and Prakash had moved on to new media consultancy challenges. I have not heard of anyone running similar courses in Australia, but there is at least one similar course now being run in the United Kingdom.

The overseas casualties of terrorism have mainly been bomb victims, such as those of the Bali bombing which killed 202 people, including 88 Australians. While the World Trade Center and Pentagon attacks (also classed as bombings) were domestic attacks against Americans, they killed a large number of foreign workers and tourists, including hundreds of UK nationals and ten Australians. What is not generally known is that the death toll was about 10% higher than officially acknowledged because of the number of 'illegals' working at the WTC whose families were not able to acknowledge them for fear that they themselves might be deported. (The September 11 attacks were classed as bombings because of the use of fully-fuelled long-haul aircraft as fuel bombs.)

Kidnappings sometimes attract greater public interest than other kinds of incident because of the human factor. Some terrorist kidnappings have been protracted. Lebanese Hezbollah held American journalist Terry Anderson for six years and British hostage-release negotiator, Terry Waite, for nearly five years in Beirut, Lebanon. Both survived their ordeals and have written books about their experiences.[35]

In March 2000, a US Federal judge awarded Anderson US$341 million against Iran, the backers of Lebanese Hezbollah. Lebanese Hezbollah was also responsible for the kidnapping of Terry Waite. Waite probably did not know that he was being used by the United States as a cover for covert negotiations that were part of what was later to become known as the Iran–Contra affair. Earlier Waite-negotiated kidnapping releases had been a consequence of arms passed to Iran by White House operative Lieutenant Colonel Oliver North. Waite spent four of his five years in solitary confinement and was released in November 1991.

Many terrorist kidnapping victims have not survived, including Australian backpacker David Wilson in 1994 in Cambodia and American journalist Daniel Pearl in 2002 in Pakistan.

The Khmer Rouge abducted David Wilson with Briton Mark Slater and Frenchman Jean-Michel Braquet, from a rural train in July 1994. David Wilson was held for ransom but there was never much prospect of him being recovered alive. To prevent the hostages' escape, the Khmer Rouge cut their Achilles tendons. David Wilson's relatives paid a ransom but it probably never reached the Khmer Rouge. More likely, government officials pocketed it. When government forces put pressure on the Khmer Rouge in September 1994, they killed the hostages, and fled the area.

Former Khmer Rouge General Nuon Paet was tried and convicted of the abduction and murder of the three men. His defence lawyer subsequently claimed they were killed on Pol Pot's orders because the ransom negotiations had dragged on for too long. The Cambodian government has reluctantly, under pressure from the foreign governments concerned, pursued prosecutions of those involved. Another senior Khmer Rouge figure, Chhouk Rin, was acquitted in 2000 and others are unlikely to face trial because of their connections within government. Those who have been convicted are likely to be released at the earliest opportunity.

Daniel Pearl was an American journalist seeking a story in Pakistan on Muslim extremism, but for an American Jew to put his trust in untested Muslim extremist contacts in an unpredictable environment like Pakistan was extremely dangerous. After his kidnapping, there was a gentleman's agreement among the media that they would not mention that Daniel Pearl was a Jew. A Pakistani journalist breached the embargo and it seems that the disclosure was Pearl's death sentence. Pearl was subsequently videoed having his head cut off while he was apparently still alive, and the video was sent to US authorities in Pakistan.

Hostage survival often depends on the reason why the person was taken. Some groups kidnap for money and, provided they eventually get some return on their investment, are unlikely to kill their hostage. Examples are FARC in Colombia and the Abu Sayyaf Group in the Philippines, who mainly kidnap foreigners to raise money. It is important that thorough negotiations are conducted by experienced hostage-negotiators to secure their release. Sometimes these negotiations may take years to conclude, during which time the hostage's health is at risk. There are however unpredictable groups like some of those in Chechnya who will extract a ransom payment and kill the hostage out of sheer malice.

An example of failed negotiation was a backpacker case in Kashmir in July 1995. The Muslim fundamentalist group Al-Faran took hostage two Britons, Paul Wells and Keith Mangan, and one US national, Donald Hutchings, and, a few days later, a German, Dirk Hasert, and Norwegian Hans Christian Ostro. Another American, John Childs, escaped. Ostro was found decapitated in August. The others were probably killed in December 1995. In January 2000, Indian forensic experts confirmed that a body recovered from a grave in Ilkingham, 60 km south of the Kashmiri city of Srinagar was that of Paul Wells. The reason they were killed, according to my Indian contacts, was the no-deals position of the Indian government. The UK High Commission had counselled the Indian Government against entering into negotiations because it would open the door to more such hostage-takings. The Al-Faran hostage-takers were seeking the release from jail in India of one of their leaders. Had the Indian Government made some concessions, the lives of the hostages might have been spared. While there are often good reasons for adopting a hard-line no-deals policy, it is not always the best way to go when lives are at risk. Past Indian practice of making concessions had meant that Al-Faran thought a deal was possible. Once they learned it was not, they saw no benefit in keeping the hostages alive.

Where hostages are taken for ideological reasons the prospects of survival are poor. Few of the Khmer Rouge's hostages ever survived, nor do many Russian troops currently survive capture by the Chechens.

The other major cause of death overseas has been armed attack—usually death by shooting. This has sometimes been in the context of an inept hostage rescue attempt. For example, local militants seized Australian Andrew Thirsk and a number of other tourists, in Yemen in December 1998. This is a time-honoured method in Yemen of putting pressure on the central government to provide local resources. In this case, diplomats of the countries whose nationals were being held pressured the authorities to do something about it. During the rescue attempt, four hostages died in the crossfire. With a better understanding of the local situation those deaths might have been avoidable.

There will always be some hazards in overseas travel but the cultural benefits generally far outweigh them. If the risks are considered sensibly and travel destinations and routes chosen on the basis of the best travel advice available, problems are largely avoidable. Indeed, one might even get better travel deals! Bali is now relatively low risk and very cheap, as is southern Algeria. Those who have no choice but to be in dangerous areas need to take local security advice and have reliable local minders to ensure that the security risks are minimised. Where their operations warrant it, such as those of UN agencies, they should maintain their own intelligence reporting to keep their staff informed of the local situation.

CHAPTER FOURTEEN

FUTURE PROSPECTS

The main concern for the future will be the activities of Al Qaeda and its affiliates. Al Qaeda is not constrained by political and societal norms in the way that a separatist terrorist group is. In that sense, Al Qaeda terrorists are more comparable to the anarchists of the 19th century than to other contemporary terrorist groups. Bin Laden's vision of a Wahhabi-like caliphate, adhering to traditional values, stretching from Morocco to Mindanao, may never be achieved, but it is a compelling vision for many Muslims who see the alternative as subjugation to what they regard as the corrupt West, led by the Great Satan, the United States.

Lack of significant progress on the Palestinian issue will continue to act as a catalyst for violence and Muslim resentment against Israel and its main backer, the United States. This resentment in turn will be used by Al Qaeda to recruit future fighters. The demographics of the Muslim-majority countries will ensure that there is a ready supply of young recruits prepared to martyr themselves for the cause.

Al Qaeda is an organisation capable of continually evolving to adapt to counterterrorism developments, which means that operationally it will be difficult to put out of business. Nevertheless, it will become more difficult for Al Qaeda to mount spectacular attacks against targets in Western countries as improving counterterrorism measures make preparations for such attacks more difficult to conceal. It will be much easier to mount attacks on US and Western interests outside those areas, in countries with poorer security, particularly in Africa, the Middle East, and parts of Asia.

If Al Qaeda's aim is to cause the US to disengage from Muslim countries, it is more likely to be successful in achieving this if it undertakes major regional operations, rather than by attacking the United States heartland. Al Qaeda can be expected to regenerate as the United States starts to focus on issues other than terrorism. It seems unlikely, based on past experience, that the United States will continue to maintain its current high level of interest in Afghanistan and Iraq, or in the war on terror. Domestic issues in the United States are likely to become more of a concern, particularly if there is a downturn in the US economy.

Terrorism will again become the major concern if Al Qaeda successfully mounts another spectacular attack in the United States. It need not be an attack causing mass casualties. Assassination of a leading Administration figure or major damage to an American icon, such as the Capitol building, would probably be equally effective in shocking the nation and maintaining current levels of US commitment to the war on terror.

However if the United States ever wants to get on top of the Muslim threat over the longer term it is going to have to pay more attention to root causes. This would require a US-imposed peace between the Palestinians and the Israelis, otherwise the Israelis will continue to play for time and build more settlements on Palestinian land. It will also require a change in the US policy of supporting unpopular leaders such as the Saudi and Kuwaiti royals, and Mubarak, Musharraf and Karzai, none of whom enjoys majority support in the countries they rule. The challenge will be in encouraging change processes that do not end up producing radical Muslim parties that will manipulate the political process to stay in power. The much vaunted democratisation of Iraq already looks like becoming a costly failure. Malaysia and Indonesia provide models for peaceful political change, despite some ongoing political and human rights abuses.

Al Qaeda's affiliates pose a different sort of security problem. In many cases they have legitimate ethno-nationalist grievances against the government of the state that they are acting against. They have obtained Al Qaeda's support because Al Qaeda supports Muslim causes, but Al Qaeda was not the cause of the violence, despite what many states with separatist problems now claim.

The war on terror has enabled many states to obtain support from the United States for their domestic war on 'terrorism', allowing states themselves to conduct acts of terrorism and abuse of human rights in the suppression of internal separatist aspirations, with relative impunity. Notable examples include China, the Philippines, and Indonesia. Resolution of these separatist situations can probably only be achieved by the involvement of honest brokers that are not seen as partisan by either side. Perhaps this suggests a more proactive role for potential peace broker countries like New Zealand—or for the establishment of regional tribunals, with both parties prepared to abide by the tribunal's decision—a sort of Judge Judy approach to internal problems!

One group that does not fit the separatist model is Jemaah Islamiah (JI) in South-East Asia because of its regional focus. Its leadership has aspirations for a regional megastate encompassing Muslim populations from several countries, the bulk of whom are in Malaysia, Indonesia and the southern Philippines. JI will be difficult to eliminate because of porous national borders and the ease with which many local officials in South-East Asia can be corrupted or pressured to allow JI activities to continue. Indonesia has a population that includes 180 million plus Muslims. Even if only one person in a thousand was to support JI or other extremist violence, that would still produce 18,000 potential activists. The approach that would seem to have most chance of success is to convince Muslims in those countries that the activities of JI or other Muslim extremists run counter to their future economic and religious interests.

We should not forget that terrorism and politically motivated violence will continue to be perpetrated by a range of elements in Western societies, ranging from single-issue extremists to loners, right-wing groups, extremist sects and anti-globalisation anarchists. Dealing with each will require different approaches. Security intelligence will remain the key defence against violence by these elements, but again, to deal with them effectively, we need to be sure that they are reflecting a minority viewpoint, rather than a majority one that should be addressed by societal change processes. Stifling popular dissent by locking up activists for lengthy periods has rarely proved an effective solution; it usually leads to further violence.

APPENDIX A

TERRORIST GROUPS

Patterns of Global Terrorism 2002
Released by the Office of the Coordinator for Counterterrorism, US State Department, April 30, 2003 *(original material courtesy of US Department of State at www.state.gov/s/ct/rls/pgtrpt/)*

Background information on designated foreign terrorist organisations

Contents

Al-Jihad (Egyptian Islamic Jihad)
Kahane Chai (Kach)
Kurdistan Workers' Party (PKK, KADEK)
Lashkar-e-Tayyiba (LT)
Lashkar I Jhangvi (LJ)
Liberation Tigers of Tamil Eelam (LTTE)
Mujahedin-e Khalq Organisation (MEK or MKO)
National Liberation Army (ELN)—Colombia
Palestine Islamic Jihad (PIJ)
Palestine Liberation Front (PLF)
Popular Front for the Liberation of Palestine (PFLP)
Popular Front for the Liberation of Palestine—General Command (PFLP-GC)
Al Qaeda
Real IRA (RIRA)
Revolutionary Armed Forces of Colombia (FARC)
Revolutionary Nuclei
Revolutionary Organisation 17 November (17 November)
Revolutionary People's Liberation Party/Front (DHKP/C)
Salafist Group for Call and Combat (GSPC)
Sendero Luminoso (Shining Path or SL)
United Self-Defense Forces/Group of Colombia (AUC)

The following descriptive list constitutes the 36 terrorist groups that currently (as of 30 January 2003) are designated by the Secretary of State as Foreign Terrorist Organisations (FTOs), pursuant to section 219 of the Immigration and Nationality Act, as amended by the Antiterrorism and Effective Death Penalty Act of 1996. The designations carry legal consequences:

It is unlawful to provide funds or other material support to a designated FTO. Representatives and certain members of a designated FTO can be denied visas or excluded from the United States. US financial institutions must block funds of designated FTOs and their agents and must report the blockage to the US Department of the Treasury.

Appendix A

Abu Nidal Organisation (ANO) aka Fatah—the Revolutionary Council, Arab Revolutionary Brigades, Black September, and Revolutionary Organisation of Socialist Muslims

Description: International terrorist organisation founded by Sabri al-Banna (aka Abu Nidal). Split from PLO in 1974. Made up of various functional committees, including political, military, and financial. In November 2002, Abu Nidal died in Baghdad; the new leadership of the organisation is unclear.

Activities: Has carried out terrorist attacks in 20 countries, killing or injuring almost 900 persons. Targets include the United States, the United Kingdom, France, Israel, moderate Palestinians, the PLO, and various Arab countries. Major attacks included the Rome and Vienna airports in December 1985, the Neve Shalom synagogue in Istanbul and the Pan Am Flight 73 hijacking in Karachi in September 1986, and the City of Poros day-excursion ship attack in Greece in July 1988. Suspected of assassinating PLO deputy chief Abu Iyad and PLO security chief Abu Hul in Tunis in January 1991. ANO assassinated a Jordanian diplomat in Lebanon in January 1994 and has been linked to the killing of the PLO representative there. Has not staged a major attack against Western targets since the late 1980s.

Strength: Few hundred plus limited overseas support structure.

Location/Area of Operation: Al-Banna relocated to Iraq in December 1998, where the group maintains a presence. Has an operational presence in Lebanon including in several Palestinian refugee camps. Authorities shut down the ANO's operations in Libya and Egypt in 1999. Has demonstrated ability to operate over wide area, including the Middle East, Asia, and Europe. Financial problems and internal disorganisation have reduced the group's activities and capabilities.

External Aid: Has received considerable support, including safe haven, training, logistic assistance, and financial aid from Iraq, Libya, and Syria (until 1987), in addition to close support for selected operations.

Abu Sayyaf Group (ASG)

Description: The ASG is the most violent of the separatist groups operating in the southern Philippines. Some ASG leaders allegedly fought in Afghanistan during the Soviet war and are students and proponents of radical Islamic teachings. The group split from the Moro National Liberation Front in the early 1990s under the leadership of Abdurajak Abubakar Janjalani, who was killed in a clash with Philippine police on 18 December 1998. His younger brother, Khadafi Janjalani, has replaced him as the nominal leader of the group, which is composed of several semiautonomous factions.

Activities: Engages in kidnappings for ransom, bombings, assassinations, and extortion. Although from time to time it claims that its motivation is to promote an independent Islamic state in western Mindanao and the Sulu Archipelago, areas in the southern Philippines heavily populated by Muslims, the ASG has primarily used terror for financial profit. Recent bombings may herald a return to a more radical, politicised agenda. The group's first large-scale action was a raid on the town of Ipil in Mindanao in April 1995. In April of 2000, an ASG faction kidnapped 21 persons, including 10 foreign tourists, from a resort in Malaysia. Separately in 2000, the group abducted several foreign journalists, three Malaysians, and a US citizen. On 27 May 2001, the ASG kidnapped three US citizens and 17 Filipinos from a tourist resort in Palawan, Philippines. Several of the hostages, including one US citizen, were murdered. During a Philippine military hostage rescue operation on 7 June 2002, US hostage Gracia Burnham was rescued, but US hostage Martin Burnham and Filipina Deborah Yap were killed during the operation. Philippine authorities say that the ASG had a role in the bombing near a Philippine military base in Zamboanga on 2 October that killed three Filipinos and one US serviceman and wounded 20 others.

Strength: Estimated to have 200 to 500 members.

Location/Area of Operation: The ASG was founded in Basilan Province and mainly operates there and in the neighbouring provinces of Sulu and Tawi-Tawi in the Sulu Archipelago. It also operates in the Zamboanga peninsula, and members occasionally travel to Manila and other parts of the country. The group expanded its operations to Malaysia in 2000 when it abducted foreigners from a tourist resort.

External Aid: Largely self-financing through ransom and extortion; may receive support from Muslim extremists in the Middle East and South Asia. Libya publicly paid millions of dollars for the release of the foreign hostages seized from Malaysia in 2000.

Al-Aqsa Martyrs Brigade (al-Aqsa)

Description: The al-Aqsa Martyrs Brigade comprises an unknown number of small cells of Fatah-affiliated activists that emerged at the outset of the current intifadah to attack Israeli targets. It aims to drive the Israeli military and settlers from the West Bank, the Gaza Strip, and Jerusalem and to establish a Palestinian state.

Activities: Al-Aqsa has carried out shootings and suicide operations against Israeli military personnel and civilians and has killed Palestinians who it believed were collaborating with Israel. At least five US citizens, four of them dual Israeli-US citizens, were killed in al-Aqsa's attacks. The group probably did not attack them because of their US citizenship. In January 2002, al-Aqsa claimed responsibility for the first suicide bombing carried out by a female.

Strength: Unknown.

Location/Area of Operation: Al-Aqsa operates mainly in the West Bank and has claimed attacks inside Israel and the Gaza Strip. It may have followers in Palestinian refugee camps in southern Lebanon.

External Aid: Unknown.

Armed Islamic Group (GIA)

Description: A Muslim extremist group, the GIA aims to overthrow the secular Algerian regime and replace it with an Islamic state. The GIA began its violent activity in 1992 after Algiers voided the victory of the Islamic Salvation Front—the largest Islamic opposition party—in the first round of legislative elections in December 1991.

Activities: Frequent attacks against civilians and government workers. Since 1992, the GIA has conducted a terrorist campaign of civilian massacres, sometimes wiping out entire villages in its area of operation, although the group's dwindling numbers have caused a decrease in the number of attacks. Since announcing its campaign against foreigners living in Algeria in 1993, the GIA has killed more than 100 expatriate men and women—mostly Europeans—in the country. The group uses assassinations and bombings, including car bombs, and it is known to favour kidnapping victims and slitting their throats. The GIA hijacked an Air France flight to Algiers in December 1994. In 2002, a French court sentenced two GIA members to life in prison for conducting a series of bombings in France in 1995.

Strength: Precise numbers unknown, probably fewer than 100.

Location/Area of Operation: Algeria.

External Aid: None known.

'Asbat al-Ansar

Description: 'Asbat al-Ansar—the League of the Followers—is a Lebanon-based, Sunni extremist group, composed primarily of Palestinians and associated with Osama bin Laden. The group follows an extremist interpretation of Islam that justifies violence against civilian targets to achieve political ends. Some of those goals include overthrowing the Lebanese Government and thwarting perceived anti-Islamic and pro-Western influences in the country.

Activities: 'Asbat al-Ansar has carried out multiple terrorist attacks in Lebanon since it first emerged in the early 1990s. The group assassinated Lebanese religious leaders and bombed nightclubs, theatres, and liquor stores in the mid-1990s. The group raised its operational profile in 2000 with two attacks against Lebanese and international targets. It was involved in clashes in northern Lebanon in December 1999 and carried out a rocket-propelled grenade attack on the Russian Embassy in Beirut in January 2000.

In 2002, there was an increase in anti-US attacks, including bombings of US-franchised restaurants and the murder of an American missionary. The perpetrators are believed to be Sunni extremists that may be linked to 'Asbat al-Ansar.

Strength: The group commands about 300 fighters in Lebanon.
Location/Area of Operation: The group's primary base of operations is the 'Ayn al-Hilwah Palestinian refugee camp near Sidon in southern Lebanon.
External Aid: Probably receives money through international Sunni extremist networks and bin Laden's Al Qaeda network.

Aum Supreme Truth (Aum) aka Aum Shinrikyo, Aleph

Description: A cult established in 1987 by Shoko Asahara, the Aum aimed to take over Japan and then the world. Approved as a religious entity in 1989 under Japanese law, the group ran candidates in a Japanese parliamentary election in 1990. Over time the cult began to emphasise the imminence of the end of the world and stated that the United States would initiate Armageddon by starting World War III with Japan. The Japanese Government revoked its recognition of the Aum as a religious organisation in October 1995, but in 1997, a government panel decided not to invoke the Anti-Subversive Law against the group, which would have outlawed the cult. A 1999 law gave the Japanese Government authorisation to continue police surveillance of the group due to concerns that the Aum might launch future terrorist attacks. Under the leadership of Fumihiro Joyu, the Aum changed its name to Aleph in January 2000 and claimed to have rejected the violent and apocalyptic teachings of its founder. (Joyu took formal control of the organisation early in 2002 and remains its leader.)
Activities: On 20 March 1995, Aum members simultaneously released the chemical nerve agent sarin on several Tokyo subway trains, killing 12 persons and injuring up to 6000. The group was responsible for other mysterious chemical accidents in Japan in 1994. Its efforts to conduct attacks using biological agents have been unsuccessful. Japanese police arrested Asahara in May 1995, and he remained on trial facing charges for 13 crimes, including 7 counts of murder at the end of 2001. Legal analysts say it will take several more years to conclude the trial. Since 1997, the cult continued to recruit new members, engage in commercial enterprise, and acquire property, although it scaled back these activities

significantly in 2001 in response to public outcry. The cult maintains an Internet home page. In July 2001, Russian authorities arrested a group of Russian Aum followers who had planned to set off bombs near the Imperial Palace in Tokyo as part of an operation to free Asahara from jail and then smuggle him to Russia.

Strength: The Aum's current membership is estimated at 1500 to 2000 persons. At the time of the Tokyo subway attack, the group claimed to have 9000 members in Japan and up to 40,000 worldwide.

Location/Area of Operation: The Aum's principal membership is located only in Japan, but a residual branch comprising an unknown number of followers has surfaced in Russia.

External Aid: None.

Basque Fatherland and Liberty (ETA) aka Euzkadi Ta Askatasuna

Description: Founded in 1959 with the aim of establishing an independent homeland based on Marxist principles in the northern Spanish Provinces of Vizcaya, Guipuzcoa, Alava, and Navarra, and the southwestern French Departments of Labourd, Basse-Navarra, and Soule. Recent Spanish counterterrorism initiatives are hampering the group's operational capabilities. Spanish police arrested 123 ETA members and accomplices in 2002; French authorities arrested dozens more. In August, a Spanish judge placed a provisional ban on ETA's political wing, Batasuna.

Activities: Primarily involved in bombings and assassinations of Spanish Government officials, security and military forces, politicians, and judicial figures; in December 2002, however, ETA reiterated its intention to target Spanish tourist areas. In 2002, ETA killed five persons, including a child, a notable decrease from 2001's death toll of 15, and wounded approximately 90 persons. The group has killed more than 800 persons and injured hundreds of others since it began lethal attacks in the early 1960s. ETA finances its activities through kidnappings, robberies, and extortion.

Strength: Unknown; hundreds of members, plus supporters.

Location/Area of Operation: Operates primarily in the Basque autonomous regions of northern Spain and southwestern France, but also has bombed Spanish and French interests elsewhere.
External Aid: Has received training at various times in the past in Libya, Lebanon, and Nicaragua. Some ETA members allegedly have received sanctuary in Cuba while others reside in South America.

Communist Party of Philippines/ New People's Army (CPP/NPA)

Description: The military wing of the Communist Party of the Philippines (CPP), the NPA is a Maoist group formed in March 1969 with the aim of overthrowing the government through protracted guerrilla warfare. The chairman of the CPP's Central Committee and the NPA's founder, Jose Maria Sison, directs all CPP and NPA activity from the Netherlands, where he lives in self-imposed exile. Fellow Central Committee member and director of the CPP's National Democratic Front (NDF) Luis Jalandoni also lives in the Netherlands and has become a Dutch citizen. Although primarily a rural-based guerrilla group, the NPA has an active urban infrastructure to conduct terrorism and uses city-based assassination squads. Derives most of its funding from contributions of supporters in the Philippines, Europe, and elsewhere, and from so-called revolutionary taxes extorted from local businesses.
Activities: The NPA primarily targets Philippine security forces, politicians, judges, government informers, former rebels who wish to leave the NPA, and alleged criminals. Opposes any US military presence in the Philippines and attacked US military interests before the US base closures in 1992. Press reports in 1999 and in late 2001 indicated that the NPA is again targeting US troops participating in joint military exercises as well as US Embassy personnel. The NPA claimed responsibility for the assassination of congressmen from Quezon in May 2001 and Cagayan in June 2001 and many other killings. In January 2002, the NPA publicly expressed its intent to target US personnel in the Philippines.
Strength: Slowly growing; estimated at more than 10,000.

Location/Area of Operation: Operates in rural Luzon, Visayas, and parts of Mindanao. Has cells in Manila and other metropolitan centres.
External Aid: Unknown.

Al-Gama'a al-Islamiyya (Islamic Group, IG)

Description: Egypt's largest militant group, active since the late 1970s; appears to be loosely organised. Has an external wing with supporters in several countries worldwide. The group issued a cease-fire in March 1999, but its spiritual leader, Sheik Omar Abdul Rahman, sentenced to life in prison in January 1996 for his involvement in the 1993 World Trade Center bombing and incarcerated in the United States, rescinded his support for the cease-fire in June 2000. The Gama'a has not conducted an attack inside Egypt since August 1998. Senior members signed Osama bin Laden's fatwa in February 1998 calling for attacks against the United States.

Unofficially split in two factions; one that supports the cease-fire led by Mustafa Hamza, and one led by Rifa'i Taha Musa, calling for a return to armed operations. Taha Musa in early 2001 published a book in which he attempted to justify terrorist attacks that would cause mass casualties. Musa disappeared several months thereafter, and there are conflicting reports as to his current whereabouts. In March 2002, members of the group's historic leadership in Egypt declared use of violence misguided and renounced its future use, prompting denunciations by much of the leadership abroad.

For members still dedicated to violent jihad, primary goal is to overthrow the Egyptian Government and replace it with an Islamic state. Disaffected IG members, such as those potentially inspired by Taha Musa or Abdul Rahman, may be interested in carrying out attacks against US and Israeli interests.

Activities: Group conducted armed attacks against Egyptian security and other government officials, Coptic Christians, and Egyptian opponents of Muslim extremism before the cease-fire. From 1993 until the cease-fire, al-Gama'a launched attacks on tourists in Egypt, most notably the attack in November 1997 at Luxor that killed 58 foreign tourists. Also claimed responsibility for the attempt in June 1995 to assassinate Egyptian President Hosni Mubarak in Addis Ababa, Ethiopia. The Gama'a never has specifically attacked a US citizen or facility but has threatened US interests.

Strength: Unknown. At its peak the IG probably commanded several thousand hard-core members and a like number of sympathisers. The 1999 cease-fire and security crackdowns following the attack in Luxor in 1997 and, more recently, security efforts following September 11, probably have resulted in a substantial decrease in the group's numbers.

Location/Area of Operation: Operates mainly in the Al-Minya, Asyut, Qina, and Sohaj Governorates of southern Egypt. Also appears to have support in Cairo, Alexandria, and other urban locations, particularly among unemployed graduates and students. Has a worldwide presence, including in the United Kingdom, Afghanistan, Yemen, and various locations in Europe.

External Aid: Unknown. The Egyptian Government believes that Iran, bin Laden, and Afghan militant groups support the organisation. Also may obtain some funding through various Muslim nongovernmental organisations (NGO).

Hamas (Islamic Resistance Movement)

Description: Formed in late 1987 as an outgrowth of the Palestinian branch of the Muslim Brotherhood. Various Hamas elements have used both political and violent means, including terrorism, to pursue the goal of establishing an Islamic Palestinian state in place of Israel. Loosely structured, with some elements working clandestinely and others working openly through mosques and social service institutions to recruit members, raise money, organise activities, and distribute propaganda. Hamas' strength is concentrated in the Gaza Strip and the West Bank. Also has engaged in peaceful political activity, such as running candidates in West Bank Chamber of Commerce elections.

Activities: Hamas activists, especially those in the Izz al-Din al-Qassam Brigades, have conducted many attacks—including large-scale suicide bombings—against Israeli civilian and military targets. In the early 1990s, they also targeted suspected Palestinian collaborators and Fatah rivals. Hamas increased its operational activity during 2001–2002 claiming numerous attacks against Israeli interests. The group has not targeted US interests—although some US citizens have been killed in Hamas operations—and continues to confine its attacks to Israelis inside Israel and the territories.

Strength: Unknown number of official members; tens of thousands of supporters and sympathisers.

Location/Area of Operation: Hamas currently limits its terrorist operations to Israeli military and civilian targets in the West Bank, the Gaza Strip, and Israel. The group's leadership is dispersed throughout the Gaza Strip and West Bank, with a few senior leaders residing in Syria, Lebanon, and the Gulf States.

External Aid: Receives some funding from Iran but primarily relies on donations from Palestinian expatriates around the world and private benefactors in moderate Arab states. Some fundraising and propaganda activity take place in Western Europe and North America.

Harakat ul-Mujahidin (HUM) (Movement of Holy Warriors)

Description: The HUM is a Muslim militant group based in Pakistan that operates primarily in Kashmir. It is politically aligned with the radical political party, Jamiat-i Ulema-i Islam Fazlur Rehman faction (JUI-F). Longtime leader of the group, Fazlur Rehman Khalil, in mid-February 2000 stepped down as HUM emir, turning the reins over to the popular Kashmiri commander and his second in command, Farooq Kashmiri. Khalil, who has been linked to bin Laden and signed his fatwa in February 1998 calling for attacks on US and Western interests, assumed the position of HUM Secretary General. HUM operated terrorist training camps in eastern Afghanistan until Coalition airstrikes destroyed them during fall 2001.

Activities: Has conducted a number of operations against Indian troops and civilian targets in Kashmir. Linked to the Kashmiri militant group Al-Faran that kidnapped five Western tourists in Kashmir in July 1995;

one was killed in August 1995 and the other four reportedly were killed in December of the same year. The HUM is responsible for the hijacking of an Indian airliner on 24 December 1999, which resulted in the release of Masood Azhar—an important leader in the former Harakat ul-Ansar imprisoned by the Indians in 1994—and Ahmed Omar Sheik, who was convicted of the abduction/murder in January–February 2002 of US journalist Daniel Pearl.

Strength: Has several thousand armed supporters located in Azad Kashmir, Pakistan, and India's southern Kashmir and Doda regions. Supporters are mostly Pakistanis and Kashmiris and also include Afghans and Arab veterans of the Afghan war. Uses light and heavy machineguns, assault rifles, mortars, explosives, and rockets. HUM lost a significant share of its membership in defections to the Jaish-e-Mohammed (JEM) in 2000.

Location/Area of Operation: Based in Muzaffarabad, Rawalpindi, and several other towns in Pakistan, but members conduct insurgent and terrorist activities primarily in Kashmir. The HUM trained its militants in Afghanistan and Pakistan.

External Aid: Collects donations from Saudi Arabia and other Gulf and Islamic states and from Pakistanis and Kashmiris. The HUM's financial collection methods also include soliciting donations from magazine ads and pamphlets. The sources and amount of HUM's military funding are unknown. In anticipation of asset seizures by the Pakistani Government, the HUM withdrew funds from bank accounts and invested in legal businesses, such as commodity trading, real estate, and production of consumer goods. Its fundraising in Pakistan has been constrained since the government clampdown on extremist groups and freezing of terrorist assets.

Hezbollah (Party of God) aka Islamic Jihad, Revolutionary Justice Organisation, Organisation of the Oppressed on Earth, and Islamic Jihad for the Liberation of Palestine.

Description: Formed in 1982 in response to the Israeli invasion of Lebanon, this Lebanon-based radical Shiah group takes its ideological inspiration from the Iranian revolution and the teachings of the late Ayatollah Khomeini. The Majlis al-Shura, or Consultative Council, is the group's highest governing body and is led by Secretary General Hassan Nasrallah. Hezbollah is dedicated to liberating Jerusalem, ultimately eliminating Israel, and has formally advocated ultimate establishment of Muslim rule in Lebanon. Nonetheless, Hezbollah has actively participated in Lebanon's political system since 1992. Hezbollah is closely allied with, and often directed by, Iran but may have conducted operations that were not approved by Tehran. While Hezbollah does not share the Syrian regime's secular orientation, the group has been a strong tactical ally in helping Syria advance its political objectives in the region.

Activities: Known or suspected to have been involved in numerous anti-US and anti-Israeli terrorist attacks, including the suicide truck bombings of the US Embassy and US Marine barracks in Beirut in October 1983 and the US Embassy annex in Beirut in September 1984. Three members of Hezbollah, 'Imad Mughniyah, Hasan Izz-al-Din, and Ali Atwa, are on the FBI's list of 22 Most Wanted Terrorists for the hijacking in 1985 of TWA Flight 847 during which a US Navy diver was murdered. Elements of the group were responsible for the kidnapping and detention of American and other Westerners in Lebanon in the 1980s. Hezbollah also attacked the Israeli Embassy in Argentina in 1992 and the Israeli cultural centre in Buenos Aires in 1994. In fall 2000, it captured three Israeli soldiers in the Shab'a Farms and kidnapped an Israeli noncombatant whom it may have lured to Lebanon under false pretences.

Strength: Several thousand supporters and a few hundred terrrorist operatives

Location/Area of Operation: Operates in the southern suburbs of Beirut, the Bekaa Valley, and southern Lebanon. Has established cells in Europe, Africa, South America, North America, and Asia.

External Aid: Receives financial, training, weapons, explosives, political, diplomatic, and organisational aid from Iran and diplomatic, political, and logistic support from Syria.

Islamic Movement of Uzbekistan (IMU)

Description: Coalition of Muslim militants from Uzbekistan and other Central Asian states opposed to Uzbekistani President Islam

Karimov's secular regime. Although the IMU's primary goal remains to overthrow Karimov and establish an Islamic state in Uzbekistan, IMU political and ideological leader Tohir Yoldashev is working to rebuild the organisation and appears to have widened the IMU's targets to include all those he perceives as fighting Islam. The IMU generally has been unable to operate in Uzbekistan and thus has been more active in Kyrgystan and Tajikistan.

Activities: The IMU primarily targeted Uzbekistani interests before October 2001 and is believed to have been responsible for five car bombs in Tashkent in February 1999. Militants also took foreigners hostage in 1999 and 2000, including four US citizens who were mountain climbing in August 2000, and four Japanese geologists and eight Kyrgyz soldiers in August 1999. Even though the IMU's rhetoric and ultimate goals may have been focused on Uzbekistan, it was generally more active in Kyrgystan and Tajikistan. In Operation Enduring Freedom, the counterterrorism coalition has captured, killed, and dispersed many of the IMU's militants who were fighting with the Taliban in Afghanistan and severely degraded the movement's ability to attack Uzbekistani or Coalition interests in the near term. IMU military leader Juma Namangani was killed during an air strike in Afghanistan in November 2001; Yoldashev remains at large.

Strength: Probably fewer than 1000 militants.

Location/Area of Operation: Militants are scattered throughout South Asia, Tajikistan, and Iran. Area of operations includes Afghanistan, Iran, Kyrgyzstan, Pakistan, Tajikistan, and Uzbekistan.

External Aid: Support from other Muslim extremist groups and patrons in the Middle East and Central and South Asia.

Jaish-e-Mohammed (JEM) (Army of Mohammed)

Description: The Jaish-e-Mohammed is a Muslim extremist group based in Pakistan that was formed by Masood Azhar upon his release from prison in India in early 2000. The group's aim is to unite Kashmir with Pakistan. It is politically aligned with the radical political party, Jamiat-i Ulema-i Islam Fazlur Rehman faction (JUI-F). The

United States announced the addition of JEM to the US Treasury Department's Office of Foreign Asset Control's (OFAC) list—which includes organisations that are believed to support terrorist groups and have assets in US jurisdiction that can be frozen or controlled—in October 2001 and the Foreign Terrorist Organisation list in December 2001.

Activities: The JEM's leader, Masood Azhar, was released from Indian imprisonment in December 1999 in exchange for 155 hijacked Indian Airlines hostages. The 1994 HUA kidnappings by Omar Sheik of US and British nationals in New Delhi and the July 1995 HUA/Al-Faran kidnappings of Westerners in Kashmir were two of several previous HUA efforts to free Azhar. The JEM on 1 October 2001 claimed responsibility for a suicide attack on the Jammu and Kashmir legislative assembly building in Srinagar that killed at least 31 persons but later denied the claim. The Indian Government has publicly implicated the JEM—along with Lashkar-e-Tayyiba—for the 13 December 2001 attack on the Indian Parliament that killed nine and injured 18. Pakistani authorities suspect that perpetrators of fatal anti-Christian attacks in Islamabad, Murree, and Taxila, during 2002 were affiliated with the JEM.

Strength: Has several hundred armed supporters located in Azad Kashmir, Pakistan, and in India's southern Kashmir and Doda regions, including a large cadre of former HUM members. Supporters are mostly Pakistanis and Kashmiris and also include Afghans and Arab veterans of the Afghan war. Uses light and heavy machineguns, assault rifles, mortars, improvised explosive devices, and rocket grenades.

Location/Area of Operation: Based in Peshawar and Muzaffarabad, but members conduct terrorist activities primarily in Kashmir. The JEM maintained training camps in Afghanistan until the fall of 2001.

External Aid: Most of the JEM's cadre and material resources have been drawn from the militant groups Harakat ul-Jihad al-Islami (HUJI) and the Harakat ul-Mujahidin (HUM). The JEM had close ties to Afghan Arabs and the Taliban. Osama bin Laden is suspected of giving funding to the JEM. The JEM also collects funds through donation requests in magazines and pamphlets. In anticipation of asset seizures by the Pakistani Government, the JEM withdrew funds from bank accounts and invested in legal businesses, such as commodity trading, real estate, and production of consumer goods.

Jemaah Islamiah (JI)

Description: Jemaah Islamiah is a South-East Asian terrorist network with links to Al Qaeda. The network plotted in secrecy through the late 1990s, with the stated goal of creating an idealised Islamic state comprising Indonesia, Malaysia, Singapore, the southern Philippines, and southern Thailand.

Activities: The JI was responsible for the Bali bombings on 12 October 2002, which killed nearly 202 and wounded 300 others and the Jakarta Marriott Hotel bombing on 5 August 2003 that killed 12. The Bali plot was apparently the final outcome of meetings in early 2002 in Thailand, where attacks against Singapore and soft targets such as tourist spots in the region were considered. In December 2001, Singapore authorities uncovered a JI plot to attack US interests in Singapore. Recent investigations also linked the JI to the December 2000 bombings where dozens of bombs were detonated in Indonesia and the Philippines.

Strength: Exact numbers are currently unknown, and South-East Asian authorities continue to uncover and arrest additional JI elements. Singaporean officials have estimated total JI members to be approximately 5000. The number of actual operationally oriented JI members probably is several hundred.

Location/Area of Operation: Following the regional crackdown against JI, it is unclear how the network has responded. The JI is believed to have cells spanning Indonesia, Malaysia, Singapore, the Philippines, and southern Thailand and may have some presence in neighbouring countries.

External Aid: Based on information from ongoing investigations, in addition to raising its own funds, the JI receives money and logistic assistance from Middle Eastern and South Asian contacts, NGOs, and other groups, including Al Qaeda.

Al-Jihad aka as Egyptian Islamic Jihad, Jihad Group, Islamic Jihad

Description: Egyptian Muslim extremist group active since the late 1970s. Merged with bin Laden's Al Qaeda organisation in June 2001, but may retain some capability to conduct independent operations. Primary goals are to overthrow the Egyptian Government and replace it with an Islamic state and to attack US and Israeli interests in Egypt and abroad.

Activities: Historically specialised in armed attacks against high-level Egyptian Government personnel, including cabinet ministers, and car bombings against official US and Egyptian facilities. The original Jihad was responsible for the assassination in 1981 of Egyptian President Anwar Sadat. Claimed responsibility for the attempted assassinations of Interior Minister Hassan al-Alfi in August 1993 and Prime Minister Atef Sedky in November 1993. Has not conducted an attack inside Egypt since 1993 and has never targeted foreign tourists there. Responsible for Egyptian Embassy bombing in Islamabad in 1995; in 1998 an attack against US Embassy in Albania was thwarted.

Strength: Unknown, but probably has several hundred hard-core members.

Location/Area of Operation: Historically operated in the Cairo area, but most of its network is outside Egypt, including Yemen, Afghanistan, Pakistan, Lebanon, and the United Kingdom, and its activities have been centred outside Egypt for several years.

External Aid: Unknown. The Egyptian Government claims that Iran supports the jihad. Its merger with Al Qaeda also boosts bin Laden's support for the group. Also may obtain some funding through various Muslim non-governmental organisations, cover businesses, and criminal acts.

Kahane Chai (Kach)

Description: Stated goal is to restore the biblical state of Israel. Kach (founded by radical Israeli-American rabbi Meir Kahane) and its offshoot Kahane Chai, which means 'Kahane Lives', (founded by Meir

Kahane's son Binyamin following his father's assassination in the United States) were declared to be terrorist organisations in March 1994 by the Israeli Cabinet under the 1948 Terrorism Law. This followed the groups' statements in support of Dr Baruch Goldstein's attack in February 1994 on the al-Ibrahimi Mosque—Goldstein was affiliated with Kach—and their verbal attacks on the Israeli Government. Palestinian gunmen killed Binyamin Kahane and his wife in a drive-by shooting in December 2000 in the West Bank.

Activities: The group has organised protests against the Israeli Government and has harassed and threatened Palestinians in the West Bank. Kach members have threatened to attack Arabs, Palestinians, and Israeli Government officials. Has vowed revenge for the death of Binyamin Kahane and his wife. Suspected of involvement in a number of low-level attacks since the start of the al-Aqsa intifadah.

Strength: Unknown.

Location/Area of Operation: Israel and West Bank settlements, particularly Qiryat Arba' in Hebron.

External Aid: Receives support from sympathisers in the United States and Europe.

Kurdistan Workers' Party (PKK) aka Kurdistan Freedom and Democracy Congress (KADEK) and Freedom and Democracy Congress of Kurdistan.

Description: Founded in 1974 as a Marxist-Leninist insurgent group primarily composed of Turkish Kurds. The group's goal has been to establish an independent, democratic Kurdish state in the Middle East. In the early 1990s, the PKK moved beyond rural-based insurgent activities to include urban terrorism. Turkish authorities captured Chairman Abdullah Ocalan in Kenya in early 1999; the Turkish State Security Court subsequently sentenced him to death. In August 1999, Ocalan announced a 'peace initiative', ordering members to refrain from violence and requesting dialogue with Ankara on Kurdish issues. At a PKK Congress in January 2000, members supported Ocalan's initiative and claimed the group now would use only political means to achieve its new goal, improved rights for Kurds in Turkey. In April 2002 at its 8th Party Congress, the PKK changed its name to the Kurdistan Freedom and Democracy Congress (KADEK) and proclaimed a commitment to non-violent activities in support of Kurdish rights. A PKK/KADEK spokesman stated that its armed wing, The People's Defence Force, would not disband or surrender its weapons for reasons of self-defence, however. This statement by the PKK/KADEK avowing it would not lay down its arms underscores that the organisation maintains its capability to carry out terrorist operations. PKK/KADEK established a new ruling council in April, its membership virtually identical to the PKK's Presidential Council.

Activities: Primary targets have been Turkish Government security forces in Turkey, local Turkish officials, and villagers who oppose the organisation in Turkey. Conducted attacks on Turkish diplomatic and commercial facilities in dozens of West European cities in 1993 and again in spring 1995. In an attempt to damage Turkey's tourist industry, the PKK bombed tourist sites and hotels and kidnapped foreign tourists in the early-to-mid 1990s. The PKK/KADEK did not conduct a terrorist attack in 2002; however, the group periodically issues veiled threats that it will resume violence if the conditions of its imprisoned leader are not improved, and it continues its military training and planning.

Strength: Approximately 4000 to 5000, most of whom currently are located in northern Iraq. Has thousands of sympathisers in Turkey and Europe.

Location/Area of Operation: Operates in Turkey, Europe, and the Middle East.

External Aid: Has received 'safe haven' and modest aid from Syria, Iraq, and Iran. Damascus generally upheld its September 2000 anti-terror agreement with Ankara, pledging not to support the PKK. Conducts extensive fundraising in Europe.

Lashkar-e-Tayyiba (LT) (Army of the Righteous)

Description: The LT is the armed wing of the Pakistan-based religious organisation, Markaz-ud-Dawa-wal-Irshad (MDI)—a Sunni anti-US missionary organisation formed in 1989. The LT is led by Abdul Wahid Kashmiri and is one of the three largest and best-trained groups fighting in Kashmir against India; it is not connected to a political party. The United States in October 2001 announced the addition of the LT to the US Treasury Department's Office of Foreign Asset Control's (OFAC) list—which includes organisations that are believed to support terrorist groups and have assets in US jurisdiction that can be frozen or controlled. The group was banned, and the Pakistani Government froze its assets in January 2002.

Activities: The LT has conducted a number of operations against Indian troops and civilian targets in Kashmir since 1993. The LT claimed responsibility for numerous attacks in 2001, including an attack in January on Srinagar airport that killed five Indians along with six militants; an attack on a police station in Srinagar that killed at least eight officers and wounded several others; and an attack in April against Indian border-security forces that left at least four dead. The Indian Government publicly implicated the LT—along with JEM—for the 13 December attack on the Indian Parliament building. The LT is also suspected of involvement in the 14 May 2002 attack on an Indian Army base in Kaluchak that left 36 dead. Senior Al Qaeda lieutenant Abu Zubaydah was captured at an LT safe house in Faisalabad in March 2002, suggesting some members are facilitating the movement of Al Qaeda members in Pakistan.

Strength: Has several hundred members in Azad Kashmir, Pakistan, and in India's southern Kashmir and Doda regions. Almost all LT cadres are foreigners—mostly Pakistanis from *madrassas* across the country and Afghan veterans of the Afghan wars. Uses assault rifles, light and heavy machineguns, mortars, explosives, and rocket-propelled grenades.

Location/Area of Operation: Based in Muridke (near Lahore) and Muzaffarabad. The LT trains its militants in mobile training camps across Pakistan-administered Kashmir and had trained in Afghanistan until fall of 2001.

External Aid: Collects donations from the Pakistani community in the Persian Gulf and United Kingdom, Muslim non-governmental organisations, and Pakistani and Kashmiri businessmen. The LT also maintains a Web site (under the name of its parent organisation Jamaat ud-Daawa), through which it solicits funds and provides information on the group's activities. The amount of LT funding is unknown. The LT maintains ties to religious/military groups around the world, ranging from the Philippines to the Middle East and Chechnya through the MDI fraternal network. In anticipation of asset seizures by the Pakistani Government, the LT withdrew funds from bank accounts and invested in legal businesses, such as commodity trading, real estate, and production of consumer goods.

Lashkar I Jhangvi (LJ) (Army of Jhangvi)

Description: Lashkar I Jhangvi (LJ) is the militant offshoot of the Sunni sectarian group Sipah-i-Sahaba Pakistan (SSP). The group focuses primarily on anti-Shia attacks and was banned by Pakistani President Musharraf in August 2001 as part of an effort to rein in sectarian violence. Many of its members then sought refuge with the Taliban in Afghanistan, with whom they had existing ties.

Activities: LJ specialises in armed attacks and bombings. The group attempted to assassinate former Prime Minister Nawaz Sharif and his brother Shabaz Sharif, Chief Minister of Punjab Province, in January 1999. Pakistani authorities have publicly linked LJ members to the kidnap and murder of US journalist Daniel Pearl in early 2002. Police officials initially suspected LJ members were involved in the two suicide car bombings in Karachi in 2002—against a French shuttle bus in May and the US Consulate in June—but their subsequent investigations have not led to any LJ members being charged in the attacks. Similarly, press reports have linked LJ to attacks on Christian targets in Pakistan, including a grenade assault on the Protestant International Church in Islamabad in March 2002 that killed two US citizens, but no formal charges have been filed against the group.

Strength: Probably fewer than 100.

Location/Area of Operation: LJ is active primarily in Punjab and Karachi. Some members travel between Pakistan and Afghanistan.

External Aid: Unknown.

Appendix A

Liberation Tigers of Tamil Eelam (LTTE) Other known front organisations: World Tamil Association (WTA), World Tamil Movement (WTM), the Federation of Associations of Canadian Tamils (FACT), the Ellalan Force, the Sangilian Force.

Description: Founded in 1976, the LTTE is the most powerful Tamil group in Sri Lanka and uses overt and illegal methods to raise funds, acquire weapons, and publicise its cause of establishing an independent Tamil state. The LTTE began its armed conflict with the Sri Lankan Government in 1983 and has relied on a guerrilla strategy that includes the use of terrorist tactics. The LTTE is currently observing a cease-fire agreement with the Sri Lankan Government and is engaged in peace talks.

Activities: The Tigers have integrated a battlefield insurgent strategy with a terrorist program that targets not only key personnel in the countryside but also senior Sri Lankan political and military leaders in Colombo and other urban centers. The Tigers are most notorious for their cadre of suicide bombers, the Black Tigers. Political assassinations and bombings are commonplace. The LTTE has refrained from targeting foreign diplomatic and commercial establishments.

Strength: Exact strength is unknown, but the LTTE is estimated to have 8000 to 10,000 armed combatants in Sri Lanka, with a core of trained fighters of approximately 3000 to 6000. The LTTE also has a significant overseas support structure for fundraising, weapons procurement, and propaganda activities.

Location/Area of Operation: The Tigers control most of the northern and eastern coastal areas of Sri Lanka but have conducted operations throughout the island. Headquartered in northern Sri Lanka, LTTE leader Velupillai Prabhakaran has established an extensive network of checkpoints and informants to keep track of any outsiders who enter the group's area of control.

External Aid: The LTTE's overt organisations support Tamil separatism by lobbying foreign governments and the United Nations. The LTTE also uses its international contacts to procure weapons, communications, and any other equipment and supplies it needs. The LTTE exploits large Tamil communities in North America, Europe, and Asia to obtain funds and supplies for its fighters in Sri Lanka.

Mujahedin-e Khalq Organisation (MEK or MKO) aka The National Liberation Army of Iran (NLA, the militant wing of the MEK), the People's Mujahedin of Iran (PMOI), National Council of Resistance (NCR), the National Council of Resistance of Iran (NCRI), Muslim Iranian Student's Society (front organisation used to garner financial support)

Description: The MEK philosophy mixes Marxism and Islam. Formed in the 1960s, the organisation was expelled from Iran after the Islamic Revolution in 1979, and its primary support now comes from the Iraqi regime. The MEK's history is studded with anti-Western attacks as well as terrorist attacks on the interests of the clerical regime in Iran and abroad. The MEK now advocates a secular Iranian regime.

Activities: The worldwide campaign against the Iranian Government stresses propaganda and occasionally uses terrorist violence. During the 1970s, the MEK killed US military personnel and US civilians working on defence projects in Tehran and supported the takeover in 1979 of the US Embassy in Tehran. In 1981, the MEK detonated bombs in the head office of the Islamic Republic Party and the Premier's office, killing some 70 high-ranking Iranian officials, including Chief Justice Ayatollah Mohammad Beheshti, President Mohammad-Ali Rajaei, and Premier Mohammad-Javad Bahonar. Near the end of the 1980-88 war with Iran, Baghdad armed the MEK with military equipment and sent it into action against Iranian forces. In 1991, it assisted the Government of Iraq in suppressing the Shia and Kurdish uprisings in southern Iraq and the Kurdish uprisings in the north. Since then, the MEK has continued to perform internal security services for the Government of Iraq. In April 1992, the MEK conducted near-simultaneous attacks on Iranian Embassies and installations in 13 countries, demonstrating the group's ability to mount large-scale operations overseas. In recent years, the MEK has targeted key military officers and assassinated the deputy chief of the Armed Forces General Staff in April 1999. In April 2000, the MEK attempted to assassinate the commander of the Nasr Headquarters—the inter-agency board responsible for coordinating policies on Iraq. The normal pace of anti-Iranian operations increased during the 'Operation Great Bahman' in February 2000, when the group launched a dozen attacks against Iran. In 2000 and 2001, the MEK was involved regularly in mortar attacks and hit-and-run raids on Iranian military and law-enforcement units and government buildings near the Iran-Iraq border, although MEK terrorism in Iran declined throughout the remainder of 2001. Since the end of the Iran-Iraq war, the tactics along the border have garnered almost no military gains and have become commonplace. MEK insurgent activities in Tehran constitute the biggest security concern for the Iranian leadership. In February 2000, for example, the MEK launched a mortar attack against the leadership complex in Tehran that houses the offices of the Supreme Leader and the President. Assassinated the Iranian Chief of Staff.

Strength: Several thousand fighters are scattered throughout Iraq, and most are organised in the MEK's National Liberation Army (NLA). Some NLA units possess tanks, armored vehicles, and heavy artillery. The MEK also has an overseas support structure.

Location/Area of Operation: In the 1980s, the MEK's leaders were forced by Iranian security forces to flee to France. Since resettling in Iraq in 1987, almost all of its armed units are currently stationed in fortified bases near the border with Iran. In the mid-1980s, the group did not mount terrorist operations in Iran at a level similar to its activities in the 1970s, but by the 1990s the MEK had claimed credit for an increasing number of operations in Iran.

External Aid: Beyond receiving all of its military assistance, and most of its financial support, from the Iraqi regime, the MEK uses front organisations to solicit contributions from expatriate Iranian communities.

National Liberation Army (ELN)—Colombia

Description: Marxist insurgent group formed in 1965 by urban intellectuals inspired by Fidel Castro and Che Guevara. Began a dialogue with Colombian officials in 1999 following a campaign of mass kidnappings—each involving at least one US citizen—to demonstrate its strength and continuing viability and force the Pastrana administration to negotiate. Peace talks between Bogota and the ELN, started in 1999, continued sporadically but once again had broken down by year's end.

Activities: Kidnapping, hijacking, bombing, and extortion. Minimal conventional military capability. Annually conducts hundreds of kidnappings for ransom, often targeting foreign employees of large corporations, especially in the petroleum industry. Derives some revenue from taxation of the illegal narcotics industry. Frequently assaults energy infrastructure and has inflicted major damage on pipelines and the electric distribution network.

Strength: Approximately 3000 to 5000 armed combatants and an unknown number of active supporters.

Location/Area of Operation: Mostly in rural and mountainous areas of north, north-east, and south-west Colombia and Venezuela border regions.

External Aid: Cuba provides some medical care and political consultation.

The Palestine Islamic Jihad (PIJ)

Description: Originated among militant Palestinians in the Gaza Strip during the 1970s. PIJ-Shiqaqi faction, currently led by Ramadan Shallah in Damascus, is most active. Committed to the creation of an Islamic Palestinian state and the destruction of Israel through holy war. Also opposes moderate Arab governments that it believes have been tainted by Western secularism.

Activities: PIJ activists have conducted many attacks including large-scale suicide bombings against Israeli civilian and military targets. The group increased its operational activity in 2002, claiming numerous attacks against Israeli interests. The group has not yet targeted US interests and continues to confine its attacks to Israelis inside Israel and the territories, although US citizens have died in attacks mounted by the PIJ.

Strength: Unknown.

Location/Area of Operation: Primarily Israel, the West Bank, and the Gaza Strip, but the group's leaders reside in other parts of the Middle East, including Lebanon and Syria.
External Aid: Receives financial assistance from Iran and limited logistic support assistance from Syria.

Palestine Liberation Front (PLF)

Description: Broke away from the PFLP-GC in the late 1970s. Later split again into pro-PLO, pro-Syrian, and pro-Libyan factions. Pro-PLO faction led by Muhammad Abbas (aka Abu Abbas), currently based in Baghdad.
Activities: The Abu Abbas-led faction is known for aerial attacks against Israel. Abbas's group also was responsible for the attack in 1985 on the Italian cruise ship *Achille Lauro* and the murder of US citizen Leon Klinghoffer. A warrant for Abu Abbas's arrest is outstanding in Italy. Has become more active since the start of the al-Aqsa intifadah, and several PLF members have been arrested by Israeli authorities for planning attacks in Israel and the West Bank.
Strength: Unknown.
Location/Area of Operation: Based in Iraq since 1990; has a presence in Lebanon and the West Bank.
External Aid: Receives support mainly from Iraq. Has received support from Libya in the past.

Popular Front for the Liberation of Palestine (PFLP)

Description: Marxist-Leninist group founded in 1967 by George Habash—as a member of the PLO— when it broke away from the Arab Nationalist Movement. The PFLP views the Palestinian struggle as a legitimate struggle against illegal occupation. The PFLP is opposed to negotiations with Israel.
Activities: Committed numerous international terrorist attacks during the 1970s. Since 1978 has conducted attacks against Israeli or moderate Arab targets, including killing a settler and her son in December 1996. The PFLP has stepped up its operational activity since the start of the

current intifadah highlighted by its assassination of the Israeli Tourism Minister in October 2001 to avenge Israel's killing of the PFLP Secretary General earlier that year.
Strength: Unknown.
Location/Area of Operation: Syria, Lebanon, Israel, West Bank, and the Gaza Strip.
External Aid: Receives safe haven and some logistic assistance from Syria.

Popular Front for the Liberation of Palestine —General Command (PFLP-GC)

Description: Split from the PFLP in 1968, claiming it wanted to focus more on fighting and less on politics. Opposed to Arafat's PLO. Led by Ahmad Jibril, a former captain in the Syrian Army. Jibril's son, Jihad, was killed by a car bomb in May 2002. Closely tied to both Syria and Iran.
Activities: Carried out dozens of attacks in Europe and the Middle East during 1970s–1980s. Known for cross-border terrorist attacks into Israel using unusual means, such as hot-air balloons and motorised hang gliders. Primary focus now on guerrilla operations in southern Lebanon and small-scale attacks in Israel, West Bank, and the Gaza Strip.
Strength: Several hundred.
Location/Area of Operation: Headquartered in Damascus with bases in Lebanon.
External Aid: Receives logistic and military support from Syria and financial support from Iran.

Al Qaeda also known as Qa'idat al-Jihad

Description: Established by Osama bin Laden in the late 1980s to bring together Arabs who fought in Afghanistan against the Soviet Union. Helped finance, recruit, transport, and train Sunni Muslim extremists for the Afghan resistance. Current goal is to establish a pan-Islamic Caliphate throughout the world by working with allied Muslim extremist groups to overthrow regimes it deems 'non-Islamic' and expelling Westerners and non-Muslims from Muslim countries—particularly Saudi Arabia. Issued statement under banner of 'the World Islamic Front for Jihad Against the Jews and Crusaders' in February 1998, saying it was the duty of all Muslims to kill US citizens—civilian or military—and their allies everywhere. Merged with Egyptian Islamic Jihad (Al-Jihad) in June 2001.

Activities: In 2002, carried out bombing on 28 November of hotel in Mombasa, Kenya, killing 15 and injuring 40. Probably supported a nightclub bombing in Bali, Indonesia, on 12 October that killed about 180. Responsible for an attack on US military personnel in Kuwait, on 8 October, that killed one US soldier and injured another. Directed a suicide attack on the MV *Limburg* off the coast of Yemen, on 6 October that killed one and injured four. Carried out a firebombing of a synagogue in Tunisia on 11 April that killed 19 and injured 22. On 11 September 2001, 19 Al Qaeda suicide attackers hijacked and crashed four US commercial jets, two into the World Trade Center in New York City, one into the Pentagon near Washington, DC, and a fourth into a field in Shanksville, Pennsylvania, leaving about 3000 individuals dead or missing. Directed the 12 October 2000 attack on the USS *Cole* in the port of Aden, Yemen, killing 17 US Navy members, and injuring another 39. Conducted the bombings in August 1998 of the US Embassies in Nairobi, Kenya, and Dar es Salaam, Tanzania, that killed at least 301 individuals and injured more than 5000 others. Claims to have shot down US helicopters and killed US servicemen in Somalia in 1993 and to have conducted three bombings that targeted US troops in Aden, Yemen, in December 1992.

Al Qaeda is linked to the following plans that were disrupted or not carried out: to assassinate Pope John Paul II during his visit to Manila in late 1994, to kill President Clinton during a visit to the Philippines in early 1995, to bomb in midair a dozen US trans-Pacific flights in 1995, and to set off a bomb at Los Angeles International Airport in 1999. Also plotted to carry out terrorist operations against US and Israeli tourists visiting Jordan for millennial celebrations in late 1999. (Jordanian authorities thwarted the planned attacks and put 28 suspects on trial.) In December 2001, suspected Al Qaeda associate Richard Colvin Reid attempted to ignite a shoe bomb on a transatlantic flight from Paris to Miami. Attempted to shoot down an Israeli chartered plane with a surface-to-air missile as it departed the Mombasa airport in November 2002.

Strength: Al Qaeda probably has several thousand members and associates. The arrests of senior-level Al Qaeda operatives have interrupted some terrorist plots. Also serves as a focal point or umbrella organisation for a worldwide network that includes many Sunni Muslim extremist groups, some members of al-Gama'a al-Islamiyya, the Islamic Movement of Uzbekistan, and the Harakat ul-Mujahidin.

Location/Area of Operation: Al Qaeda has cells worldwide and is reinforced by its ties to Sunni extremist networks. Was based in Afghanistan until Coalition forces removed the Taliban from power in late 2001. Al Qaeda has dispersed in small groups across South Asia, South-East Asia, and the Middle East and probably will attempt to carry out future attacks against US interests.

External Aid: Al Qaeda maintains moneymaking front businesses, solicits donations from like-minded supporters, and illicitly siphons funds from donations to Muslim charitable organisations. US efforts to block Al Qaeda funding has hampered the group's ability to obtain money.

Real IRA (RIRA) aka True IRA

Description: Formed in early 1998 as clandestine armed wing of the 32-County Sovereignty Movement, a 'political pressure group' dedicated to removing British forces from Northern Ireland and unifying Ireland. RIRA also seeks to disrupt the Northern Ireland peace process. The 32-County Sovereignty Movement opposed Sinn Fein's adoption in September 1997 of the Mitchell principles of democracy and non-violence and opposed the amendment in December 1999 of Articles 2 and 3 of the Irish Constitution, which laid claim to Northern Ireland. Despite internal rifts and calls by some jailed members—including the group's founder Michael 'Mickey'

McKevitt—for a cease-fire and the group's disbandment, the group pledged additional violence in October and continued to conduct attacks.

Activities: Bombings, assassinations, and robberies. Many Real IRA members are former Provisional IRA members who left that organisation following the Provisional IRA cease-fire and bring to RIRA a wealth of experience in terrorist tactics and bombmaking. Targets have included civilians (most notoriously in the August 1998 Omagh bombing), the British military, the police in Northern Ireland and Northern Ireland Protestant communities. Since October 1999, RIRA has carried out more than 80 terrorist attacks. RIRA claimed responsibility for an attack in August at a London Army Base that killed a construction worker.

Strength: 100 to 200 activists plus possible limited support from IRA hardliners dissatisfied with the IRA cease-fire and other republican sympathisers. Approximately 40 RIRA members are in Irish jails.

Location/Area of Operation: Northern Ireland, United Kingdom, and Irish Republic.

External Aid: Suspected of receiving funds from sympathisers in the United States and of attempting to buy weapons from US gun dealers. RIRA also is reported to have purchased sophisticated weapons from the Balkans. In May, three Irish nationals associated with RIRA pleaded guilty to charges of conspiracy to cause an explosion and trying to obtain weapons following their extradition from Slovenia to the United Kingdom.

Revolutionary Armed Forces of Colombia (FARC)

Description: Established in 1964 as the military wing of the Colombian Communist Party, the FARC is Colombia's oldest, largest, most capable, and best-equipped Marxist insurgency. The FARC is governed by a secretariat, led by septuagenarian Manuel Marulanda (aka 'Tirofijo') and six others, including senior military commander Jorge Briceno (aka 'Mono Jojoy'). Organised along military lines and includes several urban fronts. In February 2002, the group's slow-moving peace negotiation process with the Pastrana administration was terminated by Bogota following the group's plane hijacking and kidnapping of a Colombian Senator from the aircraft. On 7 August, the FARC launched a large-scale mortar attack on the Presidential Palace where President Alvaro Uribe was being inaugurated. High-level foreign delegations—including from the United States—attending the inauguration were not injured, but 21 residents of a poor neighbourhood nearby were killed by stray rounds in the attack.

Activities: Bombings, murder, mortar attacks, kidnapping, extortion, hijacking, as well as guerrilla and conventional military action against Colombian political, military, and economic targets. In March 1999, the FARC executed three US Indian rights activists on Venezuelan territory after it kidnapped them in Colombia. Foreign citizens often are targets of FARC kidnapping for ransom. Has well-documented ties to full range of narcotics trafficking activities, including taxation, cultivation, and distribution.

Strength: Approximately 9000 to 12,000 armed combatants and several thousand more supporters, mostly in rural areas.

Location/Area of Operation: Colombia with some activities—extortion, kidnapping, logistics, and R&R—in Venezuela, Panama, and Ecuador.

External Aid: Cuba provides some medical care and political consultation. A trial is currently underway in Bogota to determine whether three members of the Irish Republican Army—arrested in Colombia in 2001 upon exiting the FARC-controlled demilitarised zone (despeje)—provided advanced explosives training to the FARC.

Revolutionary Nuclei (RN) aka Revolutionary Cells

Description: Revolutionary Nuclei (RN) emerged from a broad range of anti-establishment and anti-US/NATO/EU leftist groups active in Greece between 1995 and 1998. The group is believed to be the successor to or offshoot of Greece's most prolific terrorist group, Revolutionary People's Struggle (ELA), which has not claimed an attack since January 1995. Indeed, RN appeared to fill the void left by ELA,

particularly as lesser groups faded from the scene. RN's few communiques show strong similarities in rhetoric, tone, and theme to ELA proclamations. RN has not claimed an attack since November 2000 nor has it announced its disbandment.
Activities: Since it began operations in January 1995, the group has claimed responsibility for some two-dozen arson attacks and low-level bombings targeting a range of US, Greek, and other European targets in Greece. In its most infamous and lethal attack to date, the group claimed responsibility for a bomb it detonated at the Intercontinental Hotel in April 1999 that resulted in the death of a Greek woman and injured a Greek man. Its modus operandi includes warning calls of impending attacks, attacks targeting property rather than individuals; use of rudimentary timing devices; and strikes during the late evening to early morning hours. RN last attacked US interests in Greece in November 2000 with two separate bombings against the Athens offices of Citigroup and the studio of a Greek/American sculptor. The group also detonated an explosive device outside the Athens offices of Texaco in December 1999. Greek targets have included judicial and other government office buildings, private vehicles, and the offices of Greek firms involved in NATO-related defence contracts in Greece. Similarly, the group has attacked European interests in Athens, including Barclays Bank in December 1998 and November 2000.
Strength: Group membership is believed to be small, probably drawing from the Greek militant leftist or anarchist milieu.
Location/Area of Operation: Primary area of operation is in the Athens metropolitan area.
External Aid: Unknown, but believed to be self-sustaining.

Revolutionary Organisation 17 November aka 17 November

Description: Radical leftist group established in 1975 and named for the student uprising in Greece in November 1973 that protested the ruling military junta. Anti-Greek establishment, anti-US, anti-Turkey, anti-NATO group that seeks the ouster of US Bases from Greece, the

removal of Turkish military forces from Cyprus, and the severing of Greece's ties to NATO and the European Union (EU).
Activities: Initially conducted assassinations of senior US officials and Greek public figures. Added bombings in the 1980s. Since 1990 has expanded its targets to include EU facilities and foreign firms investing in Greece and has added improvised rocket attacks to its methods. Supports itself largely through bank robberies. A failed 17 November bombing attempt in June at the Port of Piraeus in Athens coupled with robust detective work led to the first-ever arrests of this group; trials began in March 2003.
Strength: Unknown, but presumed to be small. Police arrested 19 suspected members of the group in 2002.
Location/Area of Operation: Athens, Greece.
External Aid: Unknown.

Revolutionary People's Liberation Party/Front (DHKP/C) aka Devrimci Sol, Revolutionary Left, Dev Sol

Description: Originally formed in 1978 as Devrimci Sol, or Dev Sol, a splinter faction of Dev Genc (Revolutionary Youth). Renamed in 1994 after factional infighting; 'Party' refers to the group's political activities, while 'Front' is a reference to the group's militant operations. The group espouses a Marxist-Leninist ideology and is virulently anti-US, anti-NATO, and anti-Turkish Establishment. It finances its activities chiefly through armed robberies and extortion.
Activities: Since the late 1980s, the group has targeted primarily current and retired Turkish security and military officials. It began a new campaign against foreign interests in 1990, which included attacks against US military and diplomatic personnel and facilities. In its first significant terrorist act as DHKP/C in 1996, it assassinated a prominent Turkish businessman and two others. DHKP/C added suicide bombings to its repertoire in 2001, with successful attacks against Turkish police in January and September. Security operations in Turkey and elsewhere have weakened the group, however. DHKP/C did not conduct any major terrorist attacks in 2002.

Strength: Unknown.
Location/Area of Operation: Turkey, primarily Istanbul. Raises funds in Europe.
External Aid: Unknown.

The Salafist Group for Call and Combat (GSPC)

Description: The Salafist Group for Call and Combat (GSPC), an outgrowth of the GIA, appears to have eclipsed the GIA since approximately 1998, and is currently the most effective armed group inside Algeria. In contrast to the GIA, the GSPC has gained popular support through its pledge to avoid civilian attacks inside Algeria. Its adherents abroad appear to have largely co-opted the external networks of the GIA, active particularly throughout Europe, Africa, and the Middle East.
Activities: The GSPC continues to conduct operations aimed at government and military targets, primarily in rural areas, although civilians are sometimes killed. Such attacks include false roadblocks and attacks against convoys transporting military, police, or other government personnel. According to press reporting, some GSPC members in Europe maintain contacts with other North African extremists sympathetic to Al Qaeda. In late 2002, Algerian authorities announced they had killed a Yemeni Al Qaeda operative who had been meeting with the GSPC inside Algeria.
Strength: Unknown; probably several hundred fighters with an unknown number of support networks inside Algeria.
Location/Area of Operation: Algeria.
External Aid: Algerian expatriates and GSPC members abroad, many residing in Western Europe, provide financial and logistic support. In addition, the Algerian Government has accused Iran and Sudan of supporting Algerian extremists in years past.

Sendero Luminoso (Shining Path, or SL)

Description: Former university professor Abimael Guzman formed SL in Peru in the late 1960s, and his teachings created the foundation of

SL's militant Maoist doctrine. In the 1980s, SL became one of the most ruthless terrorist groups in the Western Hemisphere—approximately 30,000 persons have died since Shining Path took up arms in 1980. The Peruvian Government made dramatic gains against SL during the 1990s, but reports of a recent SL involvement in narcotrafficking indicate that it may have a new source of funding with which to sustain a resurgence. Its stated goal is to destroy existing Peruvian institutions and replace them with a communist peasant revolutionary regime. It also opposes any influence by foreign governments, as well as by other Latin American guerrilla groups, especially the Tupac Amaru Revolutionary Movement (MRTA).

In 2002, eight suspected SL members were arrested on suspicion of complicity in the 20 March bombing across the street from the US Embassy that killed 10 persons. They are being held pending charges, which could take up to one year. Lima has been very aggressive in prosecuting terrorist suspects in 2002. According to the Peruvian National Police Intelligence Directorate, 199 suspected terrorists were arrested between January and mid-November. Counterterrorist operations targeted pockets of terrorist activity in the Upper Huallaga River Valley and the Apurimac/Ene River Valley, where SL columns continued to conduct periodic attacks.

Activities: Conducted indiscriminate bombing campaigns and selective assassinations. Detonated explosives at diplomatic missions of several countries in Peru in 1990, including an attempt to car bomb the US Embassy in December. Peruvian authorities continued operations against the SL in 2002 in the countryside, where the SL conducted periodic raids on villages.

Strength: Membership is unknown but estimated to be 400 to 500 armed militants. SL's strength has been vastly diminished by arrests and desertions but appears to be growing again, possibly due to involvement in narcotrafficking.

Location/Area of Operation: Peru, with most activity in rural areas.

External Aid: None.

Appendix A

United Self-Defense Forces/Group of Colombia (AUC–Autodefensas Unidas de Colombia)

Description: The AUC—commonly referred to as the paramilitaries—is an umbrella organisation formed in April 1997 to consolidate most local and regional paramilitary groups each with the mission to protect economic interests and combat FARC and ELN insurgents locally. During 2002, the AUC leadership dissolved and then subsequently reconstituted most of the organisation, claiming to be trying to purge it of the factions most heavily involved in narcotrafficking. The AUC is supported by economic elites, drug traffickers, and local communities lacking effective government security and claims its primary objective is to protect its sponsors from insurgents. It is adequately equipped and armed and reportedly pays its members a monthly salary.

Activities: AUC operations vary from assassinating suspected insurgent supporters to engaging guerrilla combat units. AUC political leader Carlos Castano has claimed that 70% of the AUC's operational costs are financed with drug-related earnings, the rest from 'donations' from its sponsors. Since December 2002, the paramilitary groups under Carlos Castano's influence have adopted a cease-fire and are exploring peace negotiations with Bogota. The AUC generally avoids actions against US personnel or interests.

Strength: Estimated 6000 to 8150, including former military and insurgent personnel

Location/Areas of Operation: AUC forces are strongest in the north-west in Antioquia, Cordoba, Sucre, and Bolivar Departments. Since 1999, the group demonstrated a growing presence in other northern and south-western departments. Clashes between the AUC and the FARC insurgents in Putumayo in 2000 demonstrated the range of the AUC to contest insurgents throughout Colombia

External Aid: None.

Background Information on Other Terrorist Groups

Contents

Revolutionary Proletarian Initiative Nuclei (NIPR)
Revolutionary United Front (RUF)
Riyadus-Salikhin Reconnaissance and Sabotage Battalion of Chechen Martyrs
Sipah-I-Sahaba Pakistan
Special Purpose Islamic Regiment
The Tunisian Combatant Group (TCG)
Tupac Amaru Revolutionary Movement (MRTA)
Turkish Hezbollah
Ulster Defence Association/Ulster Freedom Fighters (UDA/UFF)

Al-Badhr Mujahedin (al-Badr)

Description: Split from Hizb ul-Mujahedin (HM) in 1998. Traces its origins to 1971 when a group of the same name attacked Bengalis in East Pakistan. Later operated as part of Gulbuddin Hekmatyar's Hizb-I-Islami (HIG) in Afghanistan and from 1990 as a unit of HM in Kashmir.
Activities: Has conducted a number of operations against Indian military targets in Kashmir.
Strength: Perhaps several hundred.
Location/Area of Operation: Kashmir, Pakistan, and Afghanistan.
External Aid: Unknown.

Alex Boncayao Brigade (ABB)

Description: The ABB, the breakaway urban hit squad of the Communist Party of the Philippines/New People's Army, was formed in the mid-1980s. The ABB was added to the Terrorist Exclusion list in December 2001.
Activities: Responsible for more than 100 murders and believed to have been involved in the murder in 1989 of US Army Col. James Rowe in the Philippines. In March 1997, the group announced it had formed an alliance with another armed group, the Revolutionary Proletarian Army (RPA). In March 2000, the group claimed credit for a rifle grenade attack against the Department of Energy building in

Manila and strafed Shell Oil offices in the central Philippines to protest rising oil prices.
Strength: Approximately 500.
Location/Area of Operation: The largest RPA/ABB groups are on the Philippine islands of Luzon, Negros, and the Visayas.
External Aid: Unknown.

Al-Ittihad al-Islami (AIAI) aka Islamic Union

Description: Somalia's largest militant Muslim organisation rose to power in the early 1990s following the collapse of the Siyad Barre regime. Its aims to establish an Islamic regime in Somalia and force the secession of the Ogaden region of Ethiopia have largely been abandoned. Some elements associated with AIAI maintain ties to Al Qaeda.
Activities: Conducted terrorist attacks against Ethiopian forces and other Somali factions in the 1990s. The group is believed to be responsible for a series of bomb attacks in public places in Addis Ababa in 1996 and 1997 as well as the kidnapping of several relief workers in 1998. AIAI sponsors Islamic social programs, such as orphanages and schools, and provides pockets of security in Somalia.
Strength: Estimated at some 2000 members, plus additional reserve militias. Sustained significant losses at the hands of the Ethiopian military in the late 1990s, and members are now relegated to operating in small cells.
Location/Area of Operation: Primarily in Somalia, with limited presence in Ethiopia and Kenya.
External Aid: Receives funds from Middle East financiers and Western diaspora remittances and suspected training in Afghanistan. Past weapons deliveries from Sudan and Eritrea.

Allied Democratic Forces (ADF)

Description: Consists of a diverse coalition of former members of the National Army for the Liberation of Uganda (NALU) and Islamists from the Salaf Tabliq group. The conglomeration of fighters formed in 1995 in opposition to the government of Ugandan President Yoweri Museveni.

Activities: The ADF uses the kidnapping and murder of civilians to create fear in the local population and undermine confidence in the government. The group is suspected to be responsible for dozens of bombings in public areas. The Ugandan military offensive in mid-2000 destroyed several ADF camps.
Strength: A few hundred fighters.
Location/Area of Operation: Northeastern Congo.
External Aid: Received past funding, supplies, and training from the Government of Sudan. Some funding suspected from sympathetic Hutu groups.

Ansar al-Islam (AI) aka Partisans of Islam, Helpers of Islam, Supporters of Islam

Description: Ansar al-Islam is a radical Islamist group of Iraqi Kurds and Arabs who have vowed to establish an independent Islamic state in northern Iraq. It was formed in September 2001 and is closely allied with Al Qaeda. Its members trained in Al Qaeda camps in Afghanistan and now provide safehaven to Al Qaeda fighters fleeing Afghanistan. (Ansar al-Islam was designated on 20 February 2003, under EO 13224. The UNSCR 1267 Committee designated Ansar al-Islam pursuant to UNSCRs 1267, 1390, and 1455 on 27 February 2003.)
Activities: The group is challenging one of the two main Kurdish political factions, the Patriotic Union of Kurdistan (PUK) and has mounted ambushes and attacks in PUK areas. AI members have been implicated in assassinations and assassination attempts against PUK officials and claim to have produced cyanide-based toxins, ricin, and alfatoxin.
Strength: Approximately 700 members.
Location/Area of Operation: Ansar al-Islam is based in northern Iraq near the Iranian border outside Baghdad's control.
External Aid: The group receives funding, training, equipment, and combat support from Al Qaeda.

Anti-Imperialist Territorial Nuclei (NTA) aka Anti-Imperialist Territorial Units

Description: Clandestine leftist extremist group that first appeared in the Friuli region in Italy in 1995. Adopted the class struggle ideology of the Red Brigades of the 1970s-80s and a similar logo—an encircled five-point star—for their declarations. Seeks the formation of an 'anti-imperialist fighting front' with other Italian leftist terrorist groups including NIPR and the New Red Brigades. Opposes what it perceives as US and NATO imperialism and condemns Italy's foreign and labour policies. Identified experts in four Italian Government sectors—federalism, privatisations, justice reform, and jobs and pensions—as potential targets in a January 2002 leaflet.

Activities: To date, the group has conducted attacks against property rather than persons. In January 2002, police thwarted an attempt by four NTA members to enter the Rivolto Military Air Base. NTA attacked property owned by US Air Force personnel at Aviano Air Base. It claimed responsibility for a bomb attack in September 2000 against the Central European Initiative office in Trieste and a bomb attack in August 2001 against the Venice Tribunal building. During the NATO intervention in Kosovo, NTA members threw gasoline bombs at the Venice and Rome headquarters of the then-ruling party, Democrats of the Left.

Strength: Approximately 20 members. To date, no NTA members have been arrested and prosecuted.

Location/Area of Operation: Primarily northeastern Italy.

External Aid: None evident.

Army for the Liberation of Rwanda (ALIR) aka Interahamwe, Former Armed Forces of Rwanda (ex-FAR)

Description: The FAR was the army of the Rwandan Hutu regime that carried out the genocide of 500,000 or more Tutsis and regime opponents in 1994. The Interahamwe was the civilian militia force that carried out much of the killing. The groups merged and recruited additional fighters after they were forced from Rwanda into the

Democratic Republic of Congo (then Zaire) in 1994. They are now often known as the Army for the Liberation of Rwanda (ALIR), which is the armed branch of the PALIR or Party for the Liberation of Rwanda.

Activities: The group seeks to topple Rwanda's Tutsi-dominated government, reinstitute Hutu control, and, possibly, complete the genocide. In 1996, a message—allegedly from the ALIR—threatened to kill the US Ambassador to Rwanda and other US citizens. In 1999, ALIR guerrillas critical of alleged US-UK support for the Rwandan regime kidnapped and killed eight foreign tourists, including two US citizens, in a game park on the Congo-Uganda border. In the current Congolese war, the ALIR is allied with Kinshasa against the Rwandan invaders. The Government of Rwanda recently transferred to US custody three former ALIR insurgents who are suspects in the 1999 Bwindi Park murder case.

Strength: Several thousand ALIR regular forces operate alongside the Congolese army on the front lines of the Congo civil war, while a like number of ALIR guerrillas operate in eastern Congo closer to the Rwandan border.

Location/Area of Operation: Mostly Democratic Republic of the Congo and Rwanda, but some operate in Burundi.

External Aid: The Democratic Republic of the Congo has provided ALIR forces in Congo with training, arms, and supplies.

Cambodian Freedom Fighters (CFF) aka Cholana Kangtoap Serei Cheat Kampouchea

Description: The Cambodian Freedom Fighters (CFF) emerged in November 1998 in the wake of political violence that saw many influential Cambodian leaders flee and the Cambodian People's Party assume power. With an avowed aim of overthrowing the Government, the US-based group is led by a Cambodian-American, a former member of the opposition Sam Rainsy Party. The CFF's membership includes Cambodian-Americans based in Thailand and the United States and former soldiers from the separatist Khmer

Rouge, Royal Cambodian Armed Forces, and various political factions.
Activities: The CFF was not reported to have participated in terrorist activities in 2002. Cambodian courts in February and March 2002 prosecuted 38 CFF members suspected of staging an attack in Cambodia in 2000. The courts convicted 19 members, including one US citizen, of 'terrorism' and/or 'membership in an armed group' and sentenced them to terms of five years to life imprisonment. The group claimed responsibility for an attack in late November 2000 on several government installations that killed at least eight persons and wounded more than a dozen civilians. In April 1999, five CFF members were arrested for plotting to blow up a fuel depot outside Phnom Penh with antitank weapons.
Strength: Exact strength is unknown, but totals probably never have exceeded 100 armed fighters.
Location/Area of Operation: Northeastern Cambodia near the Thai border.
External Aid: US-based leadership collects funds from the Cambodian-American community.

The Communist Party of Nepal (Maoist)

Description: The Communist Party of Nepal (Maoist) insurgency grew out of the increasing radicalisation and fragmentation of left-wing parties following the emergence of democracy in 1990. The United People's Front—a coalition of left-wing parties—participated in the 1991 elections, but the Maoist wing failed to win the minimum 3% of the vote leading to their exclusion from voter lists in the 1994 elections. In response, they abandoned electoral politics and in 1996 launched the insurgency. The Maoists' ultimate objective is the takeover of the government and the transformation of society, probably including the elimination of the present elite, nationalisation of the private sector, and collectivisation of agriculture.
Activities: The Maoist insurgency largely engages in a traditional guerrilla war aimed at ultimately overthrowing the Nepalese Government. In line with these efforts, the Maoist leadership has allowed

some attacks against international targets in an attempt to further isolate the Nepalese Government. In 2002, Maoists claimed responsibility for assassinating two US Embassy guards, citing anti-Maoist spying, and in a press statement threatened foreign embassy—including the US—missions, to deter foreign support for the Nepalese Government. Maoists, targeting US symbols, also bombed Coca-Cola bottling plants in April and January 2002 and November 2001. In May, Maoists destroyed a Pepsi Cola truck and its contents.
Strength: Numbering in the thousands.
Location/Area of Operation: Nepal.
External Aid: None.

Continuity Irish Republican Army (CIRA)

Description: Terrorist splinter group formed in 1994 as the clandestine armed wing of Republican Sinn Fein (RSF), which split from Sinn Fein in 1986. 'Continuity' refers to the group's belief that it is carrying on the original IRA goal of forcing the British out of Northern Ireland. Cooperates with the larger Real IRA.
Activities: CIRA has been active in Belfast and the border areas of Northern Ireland where it has carried out bombings, assassinations, kidnappings, hijackings, extortions, and robberies. On occasion, it has provided advance warning to police of its attacks. Targets include British military, Northern Ireland security targets, and loyalist paramilitary groups. Unlike the Provisional IRA, CIRA is not observing a cease-fire. CIRA continued its bombing campaign in 2002 with an explosion at a Belfast police training college in April and a bombing in July at the estate of a Policing Board member; other CIRA bombing attempts in the center of Belfast were thwarted by police.
Strength: Fewer than 50 hard-core activists. Eleven CIRA members have been convicted of criminal charges and others are awaiting trial. Police counterterrorist operations have reduced the group's strength, but CIRA has been able to reconstitute its membership through active recruiting efforts.
Location/Area of Operation: Northern Ireland, Irish Republic.

Does not have an established presence on the UK mainland.
External Aid: Suspected of receiving funds and arms from sympathisers in the United States. May have acquired arms and material from the Balkans in cooperation with the Real IRA.

Eastern Turkistan Islamic Movement (ETIM)

Description: The Eastern Turkistan Islamic Movement (ETIM), a small Muslim extremist group based in China's western Xinjiang Province, is one of the most militant of the ethnic Uigur separatist groups pursuing an independent 'Eastern Turkistan', which would include Turkey, Kazakhstan, Kyrgyzstan, Pakistan, Afghanistan, and Xinjiang. ETIM and other overlapping militant Uigur groups are linked to the international mujaheddin movement—and to a limited degree Al Qaeda—beginning with the participation of ethnic Uigur mujaheddin in the Soviet/Afghan war.
Activities: US and Chinese Government information suggests ETIM was responsible for terrorist acts inside and outside China. Most recently, in May 2002, two ETIM members were deported to China from Kyrgyzstan for plotting to attack the US Embassy in Kyrgyzstan as well as other US interests abroad.
Strength: Unknown. Only a small minority of ethnic Uigurs supports the Xinjiang independence movement or the formation of an East Turkistan.
Location/Area of Operation: Xinjiang Province and neighbouring countries in the region.
External Aid: ETIM is suspected of having received training and financial assistance from Al Qaeda.

First of October Antifascist Resistance Group (GRAPO) Grupo de Resistencia Anti-Fascista Primero de Octubre

Description: Formed in 1975 as the armed wing of the illegal Communist Party of Spain during the Franco era. Advocates the overthrow of the Spanish Government and its replacement with a

Marxist-Leninist regime. GRAPO is vehemently anti-US, seeks the removal of all US military forces from Spanish territory, and has conducted and attempted several attacks against US targets since 1977. The group issued a communique following the 11 September attacks in the United States, expressing its satisfaction that 'symbols of imperialist power' were decimated and affirming that 'the war' has only just begun.
Activities: GRAPO did not mount a successful terrorist attack in 2002. GRAPO has killed more than 90 persons and injured more than 200. The group's operations traditionally have been designed to cause material damage and gain publicity rather than inflict casualties, but the terrorists have conducted lethal bombings and close-range assassinations. In May 2000, the group killed two security guards during a botched armed robbery attempt of an armored truck carrying an estimated $2 million, and in November 2000, members assassinated a Spanish policeman in a possible reprisal for the arrest that month of several GRAPO leaders in France. The group also has bombed business and official sites, employment agencies, and the Madrid headquarters of the ruling Popular Party.
Strength: Fewer than two-dozen activists remaining. Police have made periodic large-scale arrests of GRAPO members, crippling the organisation and forcing it into lengthy rebuilding periods. In 2002, Spanish and French authorities arrested 22 suspected members, including some of the group's reconstituted leadership.
Location/Area of Operation: Spain.
External Aid: None.

Harakat ul-Jihad-I-Islami (HUJI) (Movement of Islamic Holy War)

Description: HUJI, a Sunni extremist group that follows the Deobandi tradition of Islam, was founded in 1980 in Afghanistan to fight in the jihad against the Soviets. It also is affiliated with the Jamiat Ulema-I-Islam Fazlur Rehman faction (JUI-F) and the Deobandi school of Sunni Islam. The group, led by chief commander Amin Rabbani, is made up primarily of Pakistanis and foreign Islamists who are fighting for the liberation of Kashmir and its accession to Pakistan.

Activities: Has conducted a number of operations against Indian military targets in Kashmir. Linked to the Kashmiri militant group Al-Faran that kidnapped five Western tourists in Kashmir in July 1995; one was killed in August 1995, and the other four reportedly were killed in December of the same year.
Strength: Exact numbers are unknown, but there may be several hundred members in Kashmir.
Location/Area of Operation: Pakistan and Kashmir. Trained members in Afghanistan until fall of 2001.
External Aid: Specific sources of external aid are unknown.

Harakat ul-Jihad-I-Islami/Bangladesh (HUJI-B) (Movement of Islamic Holy War)

Description: The mission of HUJI-B, led by Shauqat Osman, is to establish Muslim rule in Bangladesh. HUJI-B has connections to the Pakistani militant groups Harakat ul-Jihad-i-Islami (HUJI) and Harakat ul-Mujahidin (HUM), who advocate similar objectives in Pakistan and Kashmir.
Activities: HUJI-B was accused of stabbing a senior Bangladeshi journalist in November 2000 for making a documentary on the plight of Hindus in Bangladesh. HUJI-B was suspected in the July 2000 assassination attempt of Bangladeshi Prime Minister Sheikh Hasina.
Strength: HUJI-B has an estimated cadre strength of more than several thousand members.
Location/Area of Operation: Operates and trains members in Bangladesh, where it maintains at least six camps.
External Aid: Funding of the HUJI-B comes primarily from *madrassas* in Bangladesh. The group also has ties to militants in Pakistan that may provide another funding source.

Hizb-I Islami Gulbuddin (HIG)

Description: Gulbuddin Hekmatyar founded Hizb-I Islami Gulbuddin (HIG) as a faction of the Hizb-I Islami party in 1977, and it was one of the major mujahedin groups in the war against the Soviets. HIG has long-established ties with bin Laden. In the early 1990s, Hekmatyar ran several terrorist training camps in Afghanistan and was a pioneer in sending mercenary fighters to other Muslim conflicts. Hekmatyar offered to shelter bin Laden after the latter fled Sudan in 1996.

Activities: HIG has staged small attacks in its attempt to force US troops to withdraw from Afghanistan, overthrow the Afghan Transitional Administration (ATA), and establish a fundamentalist state.

Strength: HIG possibly could have hundreds of veteran fighters to call on.

Location/Area of Operation: Eastern Afghanistan (particularly Konar and Nurestan Provinces) and adjacent areas of Pakistan's tribal areas.

External Aid: Unknown.

Hizb ul-Mujahedin (HM)

Description: Hizb ul-Mujahedin, the largest Kashmiri militant group, was founded in 1989 and officially supports the liberation of Kashmir and its accession to Pakistan, although some cadres are pro-independence. The group is the militant wing of Pakistan's largest Muslim political party, the Jamaat-i-Islami. It currently is focused on Indian security forces and politicians in Kashmir and has conducted operations jointly with other Kashmiri militants. It reportedly operated in Afghanistan through the mid-1990s and trained alongside the Afghan Hizb-I-Islami Gulbuddin (HIG) in Afghanistan until the Taliban takeover. The group, led by Syed Salahuddin, is made up primarily of ethnic Kashmiris. Currently, there are visible splits between Pakistan-based commanders and several commanders in Indian-occupied Kashmir.

Activities: Has conducted a number of operations against Indian military targets in Kashmir. The group also occasionally strikes at civilian targets in Kashmir but has not engaged in terrorist acts elsewhere.

Strength: Exact numbers are unknown, but there may be several hundred members in Indian-controlled Kashmir and Pakistan.

Location/Area of Operation: Indian-controlled Kashmir and Pakistan. Trained members in Afghanistan until the Taliban takeover.

External Aid: Specific sources of external aid are unknown.

Irish Republican Army (IRA) aka Provisional Irish Republican Army (PIRA), the Provos (sometimes referred to as the PIRA to distinguish it from RIRA and CIRA)

Description: Dissension within the IRA over support for the Northern Ireland peace process resulted in the formation of two more radical splinter groups: Continuity IRA, in 1995 and the Real IRA in 1997. Until its July 1997 cease-fire, the Provisional IRA had sought to remove British forces from Northern Ireland and unify Ireland by force. In July 2002, the IRA reiterated its commitment to the peace process and apologised to the families of what it called 'non-combatants' who had been killed or injured by the IRA. The IRA is organised into small, tightly knit cells under the leadership of the Army Council.

Activities: IRA traditional activities have included bombings, assassinations, kidnappings, punishment beatings, extortion, smuggling, and robberies. Before the 1997 cease-fire, bombing campaigns had been conducted on various targets in Northern Ireland and Great Britain and included senior British Government officials, civilians, police, and British military targets. In April 2002, the IRA conducted a second act of arms decommissioning that the Independent International Commission on Decommissioning (IICD) called 'varied' and 'substantial'. In late October, however, the IRA suspended contact with the IICD. The IRA retains the ability to conduct paramilitary operations. The IRA's extensive criminal activities reportedly provide the organisations with millions of dollars each year.

Strength: Several hundred members, plus several thousand sympathisers—despite the defection of some members to RIRA and CIRA.

Location/Area of Operation: Northern Ireland, Irish Republic, Great Britain, and Europe.

External Aid: Has in the past received aid from a variety of groups and countries and considerable training and arms from Libya and the PLO. Is suspected of receiving funds, arms, and other terrorist-related material from sympathisers in the United States. Similarities in operations suggest links to ETA and the FARC. In August 2002, three suspected IRA members were arrested in Colombia on charges of assisting the FARC to improve its explosives capabilities.

Islamic Army of Aden (IAA) aka Aden-Abyan Islamic Army (AAIA)

Description: The Islamic Army of Aden (IAA) emerged publicly in mid-1998 when the group released a series of communiques that expressed support for Osama bin Laden and appealed for the overthrow of the Yemeni Government and operations against US and other Western interests in Yemen. IAA's assets were frozen under EO 13224 in September 2001, and it was designated for sanctions under UNSCR 1333 in the same month.

Activities: Engages in bombings and kidnappings to promote its goals. Kidnapped 16 British, US, and Australian tourists in late December 1998 near Mudiyah in southern Yemen. Since the capture and trial of the Mudiyah kidnappers and the execution in October 1999 of the group's leader, Zein al-Abidine al-Mihdar (aka Abu Hassan), individuals associated with the IAA have remained involved in terrorist activities on a number of occasions. In 2001, the Yemeni Government convicted an IAA member and three associates for their role in the bombing in October 2000 of the British Embassy in Sanaa. The current status of the IAA is unknown. Despite the appearance of several press statements attributed to the IAA and released through intermediaries and the Internet in 2002,Yemeni officials claim that the group is operationally defunct.

Strength: Not known.

Location/Area of Operation: Operates in the southern governorates of Yemen—primarily Aden and Abyan.

External Aid: Not known.

Islamic International Peacekeeping Brigade (IIPB)

Description: One of three terrorist groups affiliated with Chechen guerrillas that furnished personnel to carry out the seizure of the Dubrovka Theater in Moscow on 23 October 2002. The suicide attackers took more than 800 hostages, whom they threatened to kill if the Russian Government did not meet their demands, including the withdrawal of Russian forces from Chechnya. Chechen extremist leader Shamil Basayev—who claimed responsibility for ordering the seizure—established the IIPB in 1998, which he led with Saudi-born mujaheddin leader Ibn al-Khattab until the latter's death in March 2002. Arab mujaheddin leader Abu al-Walid since has taken over Khattab's leadership role in the IIPB, which consists of Chechens, Arabs, and other foreign fighters.

Activities: Primarily guerrilla operations against Russian forces.

Strength: Up to 400 fighters, including as many as 150 Arabs and other foreign fighters.

Location/Area of Operation: Primarily in Chechnya and adjacent areas of the north Caucasus, but major logistic activities also occur in Georgia, Azerbaijan, and Turkey.

External Aid: The IIPB and its Arab leaders appear to be a primary conduit for Muslim funding for the Chechen guerrillas, in part through links to Al Qaeda—related financiers on the Arabian Peninsula.

Jamiat ul-Mujahedin (JUM)

Description: Small pro-Pakistan militant group formed in Indian-controlled Kashmir in 1990. Followers are mostly Kashmiris, but include some Pakistanis.

Activities: Has conducted a number of operations against Indian military targets in Kashmir.

Strength: Unknown.

Location/Area of Operation: Kashmir and Pakistan.

External Aid: Unknown.

Japanese Red Army (JRA) aka Anti-Imperialist International Brigade (AIIB)

Description: An international terrorist group formed around 1970 after breaking away from Japanese Communist League–Red Army Faction. Fusako Shigenobu led the JRA until her arrest in Japan in November 2000. The JRA's historical goal has been to overthrow the Japanese

Government and monarchy and to help foment world revolution. After her arrest, Shigenobu announced she intended to pursue her goals using a legitimate political party rather than revolutionary violence, and the group announced it would disband in April 2001. May control or at least have ties to Anti-Imperialist International Brigade (AIIB); also may have links to Antiwar Democratic Front—an overt leftist political organisation—inside Japan. Details released following Shigenobu's arrest indicate that the JRA was organising cells in Asian cities, such as Manila and Singapore. The group had a history of close relations with Palestinian terrorist groups—based and operating outside Japan—since its inception, primarily through Shigenobu. The current status of the connections is unknown.

Activities: During the 1970s, JRA carried out a series of attacks around the world, including the massacre in 1972 at Lod Airport in Israel, two Japanese airliner hijackings, and an attempted takeover of the US Embassy in Kuala Lumpur. In April 1988, JRA operative Yu Kikumura was arrested with explosives on the New Jersey Turnpike, apparently planning an attack to coincide with the bombing of a USO club in Naples, a suspected JRA operation that killed five, including a US servicewoman. He was convicted of the charges and is serving a lengthy prison sentence in the United States. Tsutomu Shirosaki, captured in 1996, is also jailed in the United States. In 2000, Lebanon deported to Japan four members it arrested in 1997 but granted a fifth operative, Kozo Okamoto, political asylum. Longtime leader Shigenobu was arrested in November 2000 and faces charges of terrorism and passport fraud.

Strength: About six hard-core members; undetermined number of sympathisers. At its peak, the group claimed to have 30 to 40 members.

Location/Area of Operation: Location unknown, but possibly in Asia and/or Syrian-controlled areas of Lebanon.

External Aid: Unknown.

Kumpulan Mujahidin Malaysia (KMM)

Description: Kumpulan Mujahidin Malaysia (KMM) favours the overthrow of the Mahathir government and the creation of an Islamic state comprising Malaysia, Indonesia, and the southern Philippines. Malaysian authorities believe that smaller, more violent, extremist groups have split from KMM. Zainon Ismail, a former mujahid in Afghanistan, established KMM in 1995. Nik Adli Nik Abdul Aziz, currently detained under Malaysia's Internal Security Act (ISA), assumed leadership in 1999. Malaysian police assert that three Indonesian extremists, one of whom is in custody, have disseminated militant ideology to the KMM.

Activities: Malaysia is currently holding 48 alleged members of the KMM and its more extremist wing under the ISA for activities deemed threatening to Malaysia's national security, including planning to wage a jihad, possession of weaponry, bombings and robberies, the murder of a former state assemblyman, and planning attacks on foreigners, including US citizens. Several of the arrested militants have reportedly undergone military training in Afghanistan, and some fought with the Afghan mujaheddin during the war against the former Soviet Union. Others are alleged to have ties to Muslim extremist organisations in Indonesia and the Philippines.

Strength: Malaysian police assess the KMM to have 70 to 80 members. The Malaysian police continued to investigate more than 200 suspected Muslim militants throughout 2002.

Location/Area of Operation: The KMM is reported to have networks in the Malaysian states of Perak, Johor, Kedah, Selangor, Terengganu, and Kelantan. They also operate in Wilayah Persukutuan, the federal territory comprising Kuala Lumpur. According to press reports, the KMM has ties to radical Indonesian Muslim groups and has sent members to Ambon, Indonesia, to fight against Christians.

External Aid: Largely unknown, probably self-financing.

Libyan Islamic Fighting Group aka Al-Jam'a al-Islamiyyah al-Muqatilah, Fighting Islamic Group, Libyan Fighting Group, Libyan Islamic Group

Description: Emerged in 1995 among Libyans who had fought against Soviet forces in Afghanistan. Declared the government of Libyan leader Moamar Gaddafi un-Islamic and pledged to overthrow it. Some members maintain a strictly anti-Gaddafi focus and organise against Libyan Government interests, but others are aligned with Osama bin Laden's Al Qaeda organisation or are active in the international Mujaheddin network. The group was designated for asset freeze under EO 13224 and UNSCR 1333 in September 2001.

Activities: Claimed responsibility for a failed assassination attempt against Gaddafi in 1996 and engaged Libyan security forces in armed clashes during the mid-to-late 1990s. Continues to target Libyan interests and may engage in sporadic clashes with Libyan security forces.

Strength: Not known but probably has several hundred active members or supporters.

Location/Area of Operation: Probably maintains a clandestine presence in Libya, but since late 1990s, many members have fled to various Middle Eastern and European countries.

External Aid: Not known. May obtain some funding through private donations, various Muslim non-governmental organisations, and criminal acts.

Lord's Resistance Army (LRA)

Description: Founded in 1989 as the successor to the Holy Spirit Movement, the LRA seeks to overthrow the Ugandan Government and replace it with a regime that will implement the group's brand of Christianity.

Activities: Since the early 1990s, the LRA has kidnapped and killed local Ugandan civilians in order to discourage foreign investment, precipitate a crisis in Uganda, and replenish their ranks.

Strength: Estimated 1000.

Location/Area of Operation: Northern Uganda and southern Sudan.

External Aid: While the LRA has been supported by the Government of Sudan in the past, the Sudanese are now cooperating with the Government of Uganda in a campaign to eliminate LRA sanctuaries in Sudan.

Loyalist Volunteer Force (LVF)

Description: An extreme loyalist group formed in 1996 as a faction of the loyalist Ulster Volunteer Force (UVF) but did not emerge publicly until 1997. Composed largely of UVF hardliners who have sought to prevent a political settlement with Irish nationalists in Northern Ireland by attacking Catholic politicians, civilians, and Protestant politicians who endorse the Northern Ireland peace process. LVF occasionally uses the Red Hand Defenders as a cover name for its actions but in February called for the group's disbandment. In October 2001, the British Government ruled that the LVF had broken the cease-fire it declared in 1998 after linking the group to the murder of a journalist. According to the Independent International Commission on Decommissioning, the LVF decommissioned a small amount of weapons in December 1998, but it has not repeated this gesture.

Activities: Bombings, kidnappings, and close-quarter shooting attacks. Finances its activities with drug money and other criminal activities. LVF bombs often have contained Powergel commercial explosives, typical of many loyalist groups. LVF attacks have been particularly vicious: the group has murdered numerous Catholic civilians with no political or paramilitary affiliations, including an 18-year-old Catholic girl in July 1997 because she had a Protestant boyfriend. The terrorists also have conducted successful attacks against Irish targets in Irish border towns. Since 2000, the LVF has been engaged in a violent feud with other loyalists that intensified in 2002 with several high-profile murders and defections.

Strength: 300 members, half of whom are active.

Location/Area of Operation: Northern Ireland, Ireland.

External Aid: None.

Moroccan Islamic Combatant Group (GICM)

Description: The goals of the Moroccan Islamic Combatant Group (GICM) reportedly include establishing an Islamic state in Morocco and supporting Al Qaeda's jihad against the West. The group appears to have emerged in the late 1990s and comprises Moroccan recruits who trained in armed camps in Afghanistan. GICM members interact with other North African extremists, particularly in Europe. On 22 November 2002, the United States designated the GICM for asset freeze under EO 13224. This followed the submission of the GICM to the UNSCR 1267 sanctions committee.

Activities: GICM members, working with other North African extremists, engage in trafficking falsified documents and possibly gun-running. The group in the past has issued communiques and statements against the Moroccan Government.

Strength: Unknown.

Location/Area of Operation: Western Europe, Afghanistan, and possibly Morocco.

External Aid: Unknown.

New Red Brigades/Communist Combatant Party (BR/PCC) aka Brigate Rosse/Partito Comunista Combattente

Description: This Marxist-Leninist group is a successor to the Red Brigades, active in the 1970s and 1980s. In addition to ideology, both groups share the same symbol, a five-pointed star inside a circle. The group is opposed to Italy's foreign and labour policies and NATO.

Activities: BR/PCC first struck in May 1999 claiming responsibility for the assassination of Labor Minister advisor Massimo D'Antona. In March 2002, the group assassinated Professor Marco Biagi, also a Labor Minister advisor. One person arrested in conjunction with the Biagi attack was released later on a technicality. In 2001, Italian police arrested a suspected Red Brigade member in connection with a bombing in April at the Institute for International Affairs in Rome. May finance its activities through armed robberies.

Strength: Estimated at fewer than 30 members; probably augments its strength through cooperation with other leftist groups in Italy, such as the Anti-Imperialist Territorial Nuclei.

Location/Area of Operation: Italy.

External Aid: Has obtained weapons from abroad.

People Against Gangsterism and Drugs (PAGAD)

Description: PAGAD and its Muslim ally Qibla view the South African Government as a threat to Islamic values. The two promote greater political voice for South African Muslims. Abdus Salaam Ebrahim currently leads both groups. PAGAD's G-Force (Gun Force) operates in small cells and is believed responsible for carrying out acts of terrorism. PAGAD uses several front names including Muslims Against Global Oppression (MAGO) and Muslims Against Illegitimate Leaders (MAIL) when launching anti-Western protests and campaigns.
Activities: Since 2001, PAGAD's activities have been severely curtailed by law-enforcement and prosecutorial efforts against leading members of the organisation. Between 1996 and 2000, however, they conducted a total of 189 bomb attacks, including nine bombings in the Western Cape that caused serious injuries. PAGAD's previous bombing targets have included South African authorities, moderate Muslims, synagogues, gay nightclubs, tourist attractions, and Western-associated restaurants. PAGAD is believed to have masterminded the bombing on 25 August 1998 of the Cape Town Planet Hollywood.
Strength: Current operational strength is unknown, but previous estimates were several hundred members. PAGAD's G-Force probably contains fewer than 50 members.
Location/Area of Operation: Operates mainly in the Cape Town area.
External Aid: Probably has ties to Muslim extremists in the Middle East.

Red Hand Defenders (RHD)

Description: Extremist terrorist group formed in 1998 and composed largely of Protestant hardliners from loyalist groups observing a ceasefire. Red Hand Defenders seeks to prevent a political settlement with Irish nationalists by attacking Catholic civilian interests in Northern Ireland. In January 2002, the group announced all staff at Catholic schools in Belfast and Catholic postal workers were legitimate targets. Despite calls in February by the Ulster Defence Association (UDA), Ulster Freedom Fighters (UFF), and Loyalist Volunteer Force (LVF) to announce its disbandment, RHD continued to make threats and issue claims of responsibility. RHD is a cover name often used by elements of the banned UDA and LVF.

Activities: In recent years, the group has carried out numerous pipe bombings and arson attacks against 'soft' civilian targets such as homes, churches, and private businesses. In January 2002, the group bombed the home of a prison official in North Belfast. Twice in 2002 the group claimed responsibility for attacks—the murder of a Catholic postman and Catholic teenager—that were later claimed by the UDA-UFF, further blurring distinctions between the groups. In 2001, RHD claimed responsibility for killing five persons.

Strength: Up to 20 members, some of whom have experience in terrorist tactics and bombmaking. Police arrested one member in June 2001 for making a hoax bomb threat.

Location/Area of Operation: Northern Ireland.

External Aid: None.

Revolutionary Proletarian Initiative Nuclei (NIPR)

Description: Clandestine leftist extremist group that appeared in Rome in 2000. Adopted the logo of the Red Brigades of the 1970s and 1980s—an encircled five-point star—for their declarations. Opposes Italy's foreign and labour polices. Has targeted property interests rather than personnel in its attacks.

Activities: Did not claim responsibility for an attack in 2002. Claimed responsibility for bomb attack in April 2001 on building housing a US-Italian relations association and an international affairs institute in Rome's historic centre. Claimed to have carried out May 2000 explosion in Rome at oversight committee facility for implementation of the law on strikes in public services. Claimed responsibility for explosion in February 2002 on Via Palermo adjacent to Interior Ministry in Rome.

Strength: Approximately 12 members.

Location/Area of Operation: Mainly in Rome, Milan, Lazio, and Tuscany.

External Aid: None evident.

Revolutionary United Front (RUF)

Description: The RUF is a loosely organised force that fought a ten-year civil war to seize control of the lucrative diamond-producing regions of the country. The group funds itself largely through the extraction and sale of diamonds obtained in areas of Sierra Leone under its control.

Activities: The RUF was virtually dismantled by the imprisonment of RUF leader Foday Sankoh in 2001; a Disarmament, Demobilisation, and Reintegration program begun in mid-2001; and the official end to the civil war in January 2002. The group's poor showing in the May 2002 Presidential elections and the possibility of prosecution if the impending UN-sponsored Sierra Leone Special Court for war crimes have further weakened organisational cohesion. From 1991 to 2000, they used guerrilla, criminal, and terror tactics, such as murder, torture, and mutilation, to fight the government, intimidate civilians, and keep UN peacekeeping units in check. In 2000, they held hundreds of UN peacekeepers hostage until their release was negotiated, in part, by the RUF's chief sponsor, Liberian President Charles Taylor. The group also has been accused of attacks in Guinea at the behest of President Taylor.

Strength: Once estimated at several thousand supporters and sympathisers, the group has dwindled to several hundred, although many of the demobilised fighters have not been reintegrated into society and could take up arms against the government again.

Location/Area of Operation: Sierra Leone, Liberia, and Guinea.

External Aid: A UN experts' panel report on Sierra Leone said President Charles Taylor of Liberia provided support and leadership to the RUF. The UN also identified Libya, Gambia, and Burkina Faso as conduits for weapons and other materiel for the RUF.

Riyadus-Salikhin Reconnaissance and Sabotage Battalion of Chechen Martyrs (RSRSBCM)

Description: One of three terrorist groups affiliated with Chechen guerrillas that furnished personnel to carry out the seizure of the Dubrovka Theater in Moscow on 23 October 2002. The suicide attackers took more than 800 hostages, whom they threatened to kill if the Russian Government did not meet their demands, including the withdrawal of Russian forces from Chechnya. The RSRSBCM—whose name translates into English as 'Requirements for Getting into Paradise'—was not known to Western observers before the seizure. Chechen extremist leader Shamil Basayev, who claimed responsibility for ordering the seizure, continues to lead the RSRSBCM.

Activities: Primarily guerrilla operations against Russian forces.

Strength: Probably no more than 50 fighters at any given time.

Location/Area of Operations: Primarily Chechnya.

External Aid: May receive some external assistance from foreign mujaheddin.

Sipah-I-Sahaba/Pakistan (SSP)

Description: The Sipah-I-Sahaba/Pakistan (SSP) is a Sunni sectarian group that follows the Deobandi school. Violently anti-Shiah, the SSP emerged in central Punjab in the mid-1980s as a response to the Iranian Revolution. Pakistani President Musharraf banned the SSP in January 2002.

Activities: The group's activities range from organising political rallies calling for Shiahs to be declared non-Muslims to assassinating prominent Shiah leaders.

Strength: Unknown.

Location/Area of Operation: Pakistan.

External Aid: Unknown.

Special Purpose Islamic Regiment (SPIR)

Description: One of three terrorist groups affiliated with Chechen guerrillas that furnished personnel to carry out the seizure of the Dubrovka Theater in Moscow on 23 October 2002. The suicide attackers took more than 800 hostages, whom they threatened to kill if the Russian Government did not meet their demands, including the withdrawal of Russian forces from Chechnya. Movzar Barayev commanded the SPIR until he was killed in the October seizure, which he led. The

SPIR has continued to carry out guerrilla operations in Chechnya under the leadership of another Chechen leader, Khamzat, whose true identity is not known.

Activities: Primarily guerrilla operations against Russian forces. Has also been involved in various hostage and ransom operations, as well as the execution of ethnic Chechens who have collaborated with Russian authorities.

Strength: Probably no more than 100 fighters at any given time.

Location/Area of Operation: Primarily Chechnya.

External Aid: May receive some external assistance from foreign mujaheddin.

The Tunisian Combatant Group (TCG)

Description: The Tunisian Combatant Group (TCG), also known as the Jama'a Combattante Tunisienne, reportedly is seeking to establish an Islamic regime in Tunisia and targets US and Western interests. Probably founded in 2000 by Tarek Maaroufi and Saifallah Ben Hassine, the loosely organised group has come to be associated with Al Qaeda and other North African extremist networks that have been implicated in terrorist plots during the past two years. The group was designated for sanctions under UNSCR 1333 in December 2000. Belgian authorities continue to hold Maaroufi, whom they arrested in December 2001.

Activities: Tunisians associated with the TCG are part of the support network of the broader international jihadist movement. According to European press reports, TCG members or affiliates in the past have engaged in trafficking falsified documents and recruiting for terror training camps in Afghanistan. Some TCG associates are suspected of planning an attack against the US, Algerian, and Tunisian diplomatic missions in Rome in January 2001. Some members reportedly maintain ties to the Algerian Salafist Group for Preaching and Combat (GSPC).

Strength: Unknown.

Location/Area of Operation: Western Europe, Afghanistan.

External Aid: Unknown.

Tupac Amaru Revolutionary Movement (MRTA)

Description: Traditional Marxist-Leninist revolutionary movement formed in 1983 from remnants of the Movement of the Revolutionary Left, a Peruvian insurgent group active in the 1960s. Aims to establish a Marxist regime and to rid Peru of all imperialist elements (primarily US and Japanese influence). Peru's counterterrorist program has diminished the group's ability to carry out terrorist attacks, and the MRTA has suffered from infighting, the imprisonment or deaths of senior leaders, and loss of leftist support. In 2002, several MRTA members remained imprisoned in Bolivia.

Activities: Previously conducted bombings, kidnappings, ambushes, and assassinations, but recent activity has fallen drastically. In December 1996, 14 MRTA members occupied the Japanese Ambassador's residence in Lima and held 72 hostages for more than four months. Peruvian forces stormed the residence in April 1997 rescuing all but one of the remaining hostages and killing all 14 group members, including the remaining leaders. The group has not conducted a significant terrorist operation since and appears more focused on obtaining the release of imprisoned MRTA members.

Strength: Believed to be no more than 100 members, consisting largely of young fighters who lack leadership skills and experience.

Location/Area of Operation: Peru with supporters throughout Latin America and Western Europe. Controls no territory.

External Aid: None.

Turkish Hezbollah

Description: Turkish Hezbollah is a Kurdish Islamic (Sunni) extremist organisation that arose in the late 1980s in response to Kurdistan Workers' Party (PKK) atrocities against Muslims in south-eastern Turkey, where (Turkish) Hezbollah seeks to establish an independent Islamic state.

Activities: Beginning in the mid-1990s, (Turkish) Hezbollah, which is unrelated to Lebanese Hezbollah, expanded its target base and modus operandi from killing PKK militants to conducting low-level bombings against liquor stores, bordellos, and other establishments that the organisation considered 'anti-Islamic'. In January 2000, Turkish security forces killed Huseyin Velioglu, the leader of (Turkish) Hezbollah, in a shootout at a safehouse in Istanbul. The incident sparked a yearlong series of counterterrorist operations against the group that resulted in the detention of some 2000 individuals; authorities arrested several hundred of those on criminal charges. At the same time, police recovered nearly 70 bodies of Turkish and Kurdish businessmen and journalists that (Turkish) Hezbollah had tortured and brutally murdered during the mid-to-late 1990s. The group began targeting official Turkish interests in January 2001, when its operatives assassinated the Diyarbakir police chief in the group's most sophisticated operation to date. Turkish Hezbollah did not conduct a major operation in 2002.

Strength: Possibly a few hundred members and several thousand supporters.

Location/Area of Operation: Turkey, primarily the Diyarbakir region of southeastern Turkey.

External Aid: Unknown.

Ulster Defence Association/Ulster Freedom Fighters (UDA/UFF)

Description: The Ulster Defence Association (UDA), the largest loyalist paramilitary group in Northern Ireland, was formed in 1971 as an umbrella organisation for loyalist paramilitary groups such as the Ulster Freedom Fighters (UFF). Today, the UFF constitutes almost the entire UDA membership. The UDA/UFF declared a series of cease-fires between 1994 and 1998. In September 2001, the UDA/UFF's Inner Council withdrew its support for Northern Ireland's Good Friday Agreement. The following month, after a series of murders, bombings, and street violence, the British Government ruled the UDA/UFF's cease-fire defunct. The dissolution of the organisation's political wing, the Ulster Democratic Party, soon followed. In January 2002, however, the UDA created the Ulster Political Research Group (UPRG) to serve in a similar capacity.

Activities: The UDA/UFF has evolved into a criminal organisation involved in drug trafficking and other moneymaking criminal activities. In January 2002, the UDA/UFF called for an end to sectarian violence; in the preceding months, the UDA had been blamed for more than 300 bombings and shootings against Catholics in Belfast. Nevertheless, the UDA/ UFF continued its attacks against Catholics, as well as those seen as a threat to its criminal enterprises. The UDA/UFF admitted responsibility for the murder of a Catholic postman in January, an attack also claimed by the Red Hand Defenders (RHD), a group used as a cover name by some UDA/UFF elements. The UDA also was blamed for a drive-by shooting that wounded three Catholics in September. Later in the year, three deaths were attributed to the group's escalating feud with the Loyalist Volunteer Force (LVF). Johnny Adair, the only person ever convicted of directing terrorism in Northern Ireland, was a leading UDA member until September when he was expelled from the group because of his growing ties to the LVF. In 2000, a feud between the UDA/UFF and the Ulster Volunteer Force (UVF) resulted in the deaths of seven men.
Strength: Estimates vary from 2000 to 5000 members, with several hundred active in paramilitary operations.
Location/Area of Operation: Northern Ireland.
External Aid: Probably obtains weapons from abroad.

APPENDIX B
ASSASSINATIONS

Heads of state or government assassinated include:

Zoran Djindjic, Prime Minister of Serbia (2003)
Laurent-Desire Kabila, President of the Democratic Republic of the Congo (2001)
Vasgen Sarkissian, Prime Minister of Armenia (1999)
Yitzhak Rabin, Prime Minister of Israel (1995)
Juvénal Habyarimana, President of Rwanda (1994)
Cyprien Ntaryamira, President of Burundi (1994)
Ranasinghe Premadasa, President of Sri Lanka (1993)
Rajiv Gandhi, Prime Minister of India (1991)
Thomas Sankara, President of Burkina Faso (1987)
Olof Palme, Prime Minister of Sweden (1986)
Indira Gandhi, Prime Minister of India (1984)
Anwar Sadat, President of Egypt (1981)
Park Chunghee, President of South Korea (1979)
King Faisal Bin Abdulaziz of Saudi Arabia (1975)
Dr Hendrik Verwoerd Prime Minister of South Africa (1966)
Ngo Dinh Diem, President of South Vietnam, (1963)
John F Kennedy, President of the United States (1963)
Ngo Dinh Diem, Vietnamese head of state (1963)
Rafael Trujillo, Dictator (1961)
Patrice Lumumba, Prime Minister of Congo (1961)
King Abdullah of Jordan (1951)
Alexander, King of Yugoslavia (1934)
Michael Collins, President of the Irish Provisional Government (1922)

Nicholas II of Russia, former Tsar of All the Russias (1918)
Jean Léon Jaurès, President of France (1914)
George I of Greece (1912)
William McKinley, President of the United States (1901)
King Umberto of Italy (1900)
Marie François Sadi Carnot, President of France (1894)
James Garfield, President of the United States (1881)
Alexander II of Russia, Tsar (1881)
Abraham Lincoln, President of the United States (1865)
Pope Pius VIII (1830)
Spencer Perceval, Prime Minister of the United Kingdom (1811)
Gustav III, King of Sweden (1792)
Peter III of Russia, Tsar (1762)
Henri IV, King of France (1610)
Henri III, King of France (1589)
William I of Orange, stadthouder of the Netherlands (1584)
Nero, Emperor of Rome (68)
Gaius Julius Caesar, Dictator of the Roman Republic (44 BC)
Philip II of Macedon (336 BC)

Other political assassinations include:
Anna Lindh, Foreign Minister of Sweden (2003)
Mohammed Ahmad al-Rasheed, Saudi Arabian ambassador to the Ivory Coast (2003)
Abdul Qadir, Vice President of Afghanistan (2002)
Pim Fortuyn, party leader and prime ministerial candidate in the Netherlands (2002)
Ahmed Shah Massoud, leader of the Northern Alliance in Afghanistan (2001)
Theys Eluay, West Papuan political leader (2001)
Andrey Lukanov, former Prime Minister of Bulgaria (1996)
Ian Gow, British Conservative politician (1990)
Earl Mountbatten, British statesman (1979)
Airey Neave, British Conservative politician (1979)

Aldo Moro, former Italian Prime Minister (1978)
Georgi Markov, Bulgarian dissident (1978)
Harvey Milk, gay rights campaigner and city supervisor of San Francisco, California (1978)
Christopher Ewart-Biggs, British ambassador to Ireland (1976)
Pierre Laporte, Vice-Premier and Cabinet Minister of Quebec, Canada (1970)
Tom Mboya, African politician (1969)
Robert F Kennedy, former Attorney General of the United States (1968)
Martin Luther King Jr, civil rights leader in the United States (1968)
Ernesto Che Guevara, Cuban revolutionary (1967)
Malcolm X, civil rights leader in the United States (1965)
Patrice Lumumba, African politician (1961)
Sir Henry Gurney, High Commissioner of Malaya (1951)
Mohandas Gandhi (also known as Mahatma), Indian political and spiritual leader (1948)
Reinhard Heydrich, Nazi military governor of Bohemia and Moravia (1942)
Leon Trotsky, communist and founder of the Red Army (1940)
Huey Pierce Long, US labour leader (1935)
Engelbert Dolfuss, Austrian Chancellor (1934)
Pancho Villa, Mexican revolutionary (1923)
Emiliano Zapata, Mexican revolutionary leader (1919)
Grigori Efimovich Rasputin,influential associate of the Tsar of Russia (1916)
Franz Ferdinand of Austria, Archduke and heir to the Austro-Hungarian throne (1914)
Elisabeth, Empress of Austria, Queen of Hungary (1898)
Lord Frederick Cavendish, Chief Secretary for Ireland (1882)
TH Burke, Under Secretary for Ireland (1882)
Thomas D'Arcy McGee, Canadian member of Parliament (1868)
Charles Lenox Richardson, English diplomat (1862)
Henry Heusken, American diplomat (accompanying Townsend Harris from Amsterdam) (1861)
Jean-Paul Marat, French politician (1793)
Germanicus, Roman military leader (20)

Appendix B

Those who survived assassination attempts include:

Bertrand Delanoë, Mayor of Paris, France (2002)
Hamid Karzai, President of Afghanistan (2002)
Uday Hussein, son of Saddam Hussein (1996)
Jean Chrétien, Prime Minister of Canada (1995)
Bill Clinton, President of the United States (1994)
Margaret Thatcher and the British cabinet (1987)
Pope John Paul II (1981)
Ronald Reagan, President of the United States (1981)
Gerald Ford, President of the United States (twice in 1975)
Joseph Sieff, honorary Vice-President of the British Zionist Federation (1973)
Pope Paul VI (1970)
Harry S Truman, President of the United States (1950)
Adolf Hitler, German dictator (1944)
Franklin Roosevelt, President of the United States (1933)
Alfonso XIII of Spain (1905, 1906)
Emile Loubet, President of France (1905—same attempt as on King Alfonso of Spain, above)
Theodore Roosevelt, President of the United States (1902 and 1912 after leaving office)
Edward VII of the United Kingdom, as Prince of Wales (1900)
Andrew Jackson, President of the United States (1835)
Queen Victoria of the United Kingdom (numerous attempts)
George Washington, General (1776)
Louis XV of France (1757)
Qin Shi Huang Di, Chinese Emperor (227 BC)

Suspicious deaths include:

Pope John Paul I (1978)
Salvador Allende, President of Chile (1973)
Dag Hammarskjöld, United Nations Secretary General (1961)
Napoleon Bonaparte (1821)

Charles XII, King of Sweden (1718)
Pope Alexander VI (1503)

Many assassins are not known, but listed below are those that are, in alphabetical order by surname:

Mehmet Ali Agca—failed assassin of Pope John Paul II
Yigal Amir—assassin of Israeli Prime Minister Yitzhak Rabin
Jacob Johan Anckarström—assassin of King Gustav III of Sweden
John Bellingham—assassin of British Prime Minister Spencer Perceval
John Wilkes Booth—assassin of US President Abraham Lincoln
Arthur Herman Bremer—would-be-assassin of George Wallace, Governor of Alabama
Brutus and associates—assassins of Julius Caesar
Carlos the Jackal—would-be-assassin of Joseph Sieff
Sante Jeronimo Caserio—assassin of the French President Marie François Sadi Carnot
Jacques Clément—assassin of King Henri III of France
Charlotte Corday—assassin of Jean-Paul Marat
Leon Czolgosz—assassin of US President William McKinley
Dingaan and Mhlangana—assassins of Shaka, king of the Zulus
John Felton—assassin of George Villiers, Duke of Buckingham
Lynette 'Squeaky' Fromme—apparent would-be-assassin of US President Gerald Ford
Balthazar Gérards—assassin of William I of Orange
Naturam Godse—assassin of Mahatma Gandhi
Volkert van der Graaf—assassin of Pim Fortuyn
Charles J Guiteau—assassin of US President James Garfield
John W Hinckley, Jr—would-be-assassin of US President Ronald Reagan
Jin Ke—failed assassin of the first Chinese emperor Qin Shi Huang Di
Luigi Lucheni—assassin of Elisabeth of Austria
Ramon Mercader—assassin of Leon Trotsky
Sarah Jane Moore—would-be-assassin of US President Gerald Ford
Lee Harvey Oswald—assumed assassin of US President John F Kennedy

Appendix B

Lewis Powell or Lewis Paine—would-be-assassin of US Secretary of State William Seward

Gavrilo Princip—the Serbian nationalist who killed Franz Ferdinand, Archduke of Austria and hence triggered World War I

Ravaillac—fanatic assassin of Henry IV of France

James Earl Ray—confessed to the shooting of Martin Luther King Jr

Jack Ruby—assassin of Lee Harvey Oswald

Miles Sindercombe—leader of would-be-assassins of Oliver Cromwell

Beant Singh and Sukhwant Singh—assassins of Prime Minister of India Indira Gandhi

Sirhan B Sirhan—assassin of Robert F Kennedy

Phil Strauss—Mafia hitman

Soghomon Tehlirian—assassin of Talaat Pasha

Raoul Villain—assassin of Jean Jaures

Carl Weiss—assassin of Huey Long

Dan White—assassin of Mayor of San Francisco George Moscone and Councilman Harvey Milk

Giuseppe Zangara, assassin of Anton Chermak, mayor of Chicago and would-be-assassin of US President Franklin Delano Roosevelt

APPENDIX C

SUGGESTED CONTENT FOR AN OVERSEAS SECURITY THREAT ASSESSMENT

Title
Latest date of information
Summary of threat levels
Contact person (author of the assessment)
Map of area
Introduction with 'Aim' and reason for production

Content to include:
- The military threat
- The terrorist threat
- WMD & CBRN
- Dissident/insurgent activity

Law and order situation, including:
- Prospect for civil unrest
- Criminal activity
- Organised crime
- Random violence
- Crime targeting foreigners
- Police effectiveness

• Ethnic, sectarian, factional or tribal conflict
• Corruption factors

Politically motivated violence situation
Issue motivated groups
Dangerous times/areas to be avoided
Any other sources of human threat

Third country foreign intelligence services operating in-country
Local intelligence and security services

Unexploded ordnance
Mines and booby traps
Contamination issues
Health environment
Endemic diseases
Epidemics

Civil infrastructure
Public utilities
Evacuation capabilities
Water supply/accommodation
Pollution

Cultural and language differences
Attitude to foreigners
Surface and air transport, road and driving conditions

APPENDIX D
ADVICE FOR TRAVELLERS

A useful acronym is ACME. This stands for:

- **Awareness** of your environment (as in recognise a bad situation and avoid it—not a good idea to hear gunfire and go and take a look to see what's happening)
- **Consider** your options (someone asks you to carry something across a border for them—not a good idea because it may not be what you were told it is)
- **Mitigate** by backing down (avoid a nasty situation by being friendly, handing over something as a gift, in the last resort, your wallet),
- **Extract** yourself from danger (in other words, get out of the danger area as rapidly as possible—go bush if you have to).

It is always a good idea to carry a duplicate wallet with minimal cash and expired credit cards, and to hide your real wallet.

Always have a travel plan and let someone know where you are going to be; at least in general terms. Make the effort to keep in touch so that if you suddenly disappear it will be possible to start search procedures with some degree of surety as to where you might be. To head off into rural Peru for several months without making at least basic plans or having contact arrangements is asking for trouble. I once traveled from Panama to Colombia and opted (after looking at the alternatives) to fly. Not very adventurous, but the alternatives were to take a smuggler's boat along the coast or walk through the jungle for a few days. There is no law in those areas and no accountability. People there are poor and what most backpackers are carrying is worth more than their possessions. If someone killed you, they would not be held accountable. Each year, several backpackers disappear in that area.

Being aware of the culture is important so that you do not offend the locals. This is particularly relevant in Muslim countries where women are not permitted to wear Western dress. Western girls traveling alone in Muslim countries are often thought to be prostitutes. In any case, if you are offensive to the locals you will not be well treated or have a positive cultural experience and you might as well have stayed at home.

It is a good idea to check the weather situation for the area you are going to. Burma in the monsoon period is rather a waste of time, even though the rates might be cheaper. And of course there is the danger in some places, like Bangladesh and South America, of mudslides and floods. Other places suffer hurricanes, typhoons and earthquakes—all of which can ruin your travel experience.

The health situation can be checked on by visiting the World Health Organisation site at www.who.org. There is nothing more likely to make you wish you had stayed at home than getting sick. I got amoebic dysentery in Colombia from a fast food joint hamburger lettuce. The only efficient healthcare providers there are the military and the church. You can dehydrate very quickly from vomiting and 'the runs'. Even Lomotil (handy for most stomach upsets) was ineffective against amoebic dysentery. It was not until I returned to the United States and was treated with sulphur drugs that my health was restored. The WHO is also a good source of information about disease outbreaks and areas to be avoided.

Some other health tips are to have your teeth sorted out before you travel, know your blood group and ensure that your travel companion knows it, and get all the vaccinations you need. Always carry a basic medical kit in your carry bag. If your bus crashes you may not have access to your backpack. Know basic first aid before you travel. For example, know when to apply a pressure bandage and how to treat shock.

Always get health and travel insurance. Water is always an issue given the number of waterborne diseases, therefore don't sing in the shower! Never use local ice.

Other administrative needs are to check your passport validity (it should have at least 12 months currency) and visas. Sometimes it pays to use two passports where the cost of a visa on one may be cheaper than the other, or may not even be needed. For example, it is better to travel on a British passport in South America, where visas are generally not required by UK passport holders, than on an Australian one. Be aware though that if you travel to your country of birth on its passport, it may be difficult for you to get consular support from your country of residence if you get into trouble. Australian nationals with dual nationality must always enter Australia using their Australian passport.

Some other suggestions. Always arrive in a new location with pre-booked accommodation so that you can get a feel for the place. Avoid hotels near bus and railway stations—they tend to attract low life. Arrive during daylight hours. Do not take an unregistered cab—it is a recipe for being robbed. Do not sleep on the beach—it can be a health hazard as well as exposing you to criminal attack. Obviously if you are part of a large group you can use your judgment about where you sleep, but it is generally not a good idea to camp on your own, certainly not in South or Central America, or Indonesia.

There are of course reams of safety and security advice that one can provide. Ten useful tips are:

- Research the place you are going to.
- Copy documents digitally and email them to your hotmail or yahoo account as back-up.
- Dress down—and avoid clothing with US flags etc.
- Look confident—the best defence.
- If sick, drink lots of water or flat Coke and stay out of the sun.
- Stick to bottled water and check the seal.
- Fit in with local customs.
- Trust your instincts—if a situation feels bad, leave.
- Stay in touch with someone, perhaps through mobile phone text messages.
- Leave valuables at home—don't travel with attractive items.

ENDNOTES

1. Ian Robertson, *Sociology*, Third Edition, Worth Publishers Inc, 1987, p. 556.
2. There are numerous examples of politically motivated individuals acting alone to try to achieve some desired outcome. They often have had no contact with others holding the same views, but may have absorbed a compatible ideology from reading information disseminated by a group. Also referred to as 'mavericks'.
3. '18' is sometimes used by Nazi groups as a substitute for 'A' and 'H' from Adolf Hitler, being the first and eighth letters of the alphabet.
4. There have been several leaks of Australian Defence documents in recent years highlighting the differences between what the Australian Government said it knew, and what it actually knew.
5. These include, *Living with Terrorism*, Faber & Faber, 1975, *Guerrillas and Terrorists*, Ohio Univ Press, 1980, *Kidnap, Hijack and Extortion: The Response*, Palgrave Macmillan, 1987 and *Terrorism and Guerrilla Warfare: Forecasts and Remedies*, Routledge, 1990.
6. Mark V. Kauppi, 'Terrorist Motivation', Counterterrorism Training Program, Joint Military. Intelligence Training Center, March 2000.
7. Bakunin's writings were widely scattered and he never organised any of them into finished books. Max Nettlau and E H Carr have written authoritative biographies of Bakunin, while G P Maximoff has made a partial collection of his works published by The Free Press.
8. Michael Vatikiotis, 'A Tale of Two Madrasas', *Far Eastern Economic Review*, 27 June 2002, p. 60.
9. Ehud Sprinzak, 'Rational Fanatics', *Foreign Policy*, Sep/Oct 2001.
10. See Martha Crenshaw, 'How Terrorism Ends', *Terrorism and Politically Motivated Violence*, Vol 3, No 1 Spring 1991, pp. 69–87.
11. US State Department, *Patterns of Global Terrorism* 2002, April 2003.
12. The list will be updated at the end of April 2004 when *Patterns of Global Terrorism 2003* is released (see http://www.state.gov/s/ct/rls/pgtrpt/)

13. US State Department, *Patterns of Global Terrorism* 2002, April 2003.
14. For further information on cults see: http://www.religioustolerance.org/destruct.html
15. The Taliban practises Deobandism, which also takes Islam back to its basics.
16. By contrast, 'fundamentalists' do not necessarily support violent approaches.
17. Details of these groups, and others, are included in Appendix A.
18. IISS, *Strategic Comments*, Vol 9 Issue 4 2003.
19. Barton Gellman, 'Cyber-Attacks by Al Qaeda Feared, *The Washington Post*, 27 June 2002.
20. See Cliff Saran, 'Why are we in this mess?', *Computer Weekly*, 31 July 2001.
21. Jeordan Legon, 'As Net attack eases, blame game surges', CNN, 28 January 2003.
22. See the Hackers Dictionary http://www.mcs.kent.edu/docs/general/hackersdict/
23. Technically, to crash a program by overrunning a fixed-size buffer with excessively large input data.
24. A logic bomb is Code surreptitiously inserted into an application or operating system that causes it to perform some destructive or security-compromising activity whenever specified conditions are met. A Trojan Horse is a malicious, security-breaking program that is disguised as something benign, such as a directory lister, archiver, game, or a program to find and destroy viruses. See The New Hacker's Dictionary http://people.kldp.org/~eunjea/jargon/
25. A form of Denial of Service attack consisting of a flood of 'ping' requests (normally used to check network conditions) designed to disrupt the normal activity of a system. This act is sometimes called ping lashing or ping flood.
26. An attack may originate in Russia and strike via South Africa, South Korea and perhaps a number of hard to check way-points.
27. See http://www.wikipedia.org/wiki/Assassination
28. Israel under Sharon is continuing to build settlements in the West Bank and seems to be working toward absorption of much of the West Bank. 250,000 Israeli settlers now live in the occupied territories. Israel is in clear breach of international agreements

and is able to avoid being brought to account by US political, economic and military support.

29. For texts see www.auslii.edu.au/au/other/dfat/OAS
30. Australian Government Protective Security Manual 2000, known as PSM 2000. It is not available to the public but can be made available to security personnel. (An updated version is due out in June 2004.)
31. Note the Australian Risk Management Standard 4360. A useful introductory reference is SAA HB142-1999, *A basic introduction to managing risk* from Standards Australia, produced in 1999. A more detailed approach is contained in AS/NZ 4360:1999, *Risk management* also from Standards Australia, produced in 1999.
32. 'Business' is any activity undertaken by any organisation, public or private. A useful reference is a booklet titled *Non-stop service*, by Emergency Management Australia, produced in 1997. A new handbook on business continuity should be available from Standards Australia in May 2004.
33. For English language travel advisories see US = http://travel.state.gov.travel_warnings.html; UK = http://www.fco.gov.uk and access 'Travel Advice and Travellers' Tips'; Australia = http://www.dfat.gov.au/travel/index.html; Canada = http://www.voyage.gc.ca/dest/index.asp
34. www.lonelyplanet.com/travel_ticker/travel_advisories.html
35. Terry Anderson, *Den of Lions: Memories of Seven Years*, Terry Waite, *Taken on Trust*, both available from Amazon Books.

INDEX

Index

Index

Index